SQUEAKY SNEAKERS

Life Lessons Learned on the Hardwood

because ball really is life!

Layne Allen Fields

Copyright

Published by Doing Small Better
First Edition

Disclaimer: The content in this book is for inspirational and educational purposes only and is not intended as legal, financial, medical, or professional advice.

Scripture Usage (if applicable): Unless otherwise noted, Scripture quotations are from the New King James Version® (NKJV®). Copyright © 1982 by Thomas Nelson. Used by permission.

ISBN: 979-8-218-91616-9

Printed in the United States of America

Dedicated to

Sydney and Spencer

My life took on new meaning when you entered the world. Everything I do, and everything I have done, has been to give you the best life possible.

Every sacrifice, every decision, and every standard I chose to live by was made with you in mind.

I tried to play the game of life the right way, knowing you were in the stands watching. I hope my play resulted in you two as my biggest fans.

Dad

GAME PLAN

The Coach's Office
Starting Lineup
Jump Ball

1st Quarter – Foundation & Character

    1st POSSESSION — Be Available
    2nd POSSESSION — Listen to The Coach
    3rd POSSESSION — Discipline Over Talent
    4th POSSESSION — Fundamentals Before Flash
    5th POSSESSION — Protect The Ball
    6th POSSESSION — No Compound Mistakes
    7th POSSESSION — Have a Short Memory
    8th POSSESSION — Play Inside Out
    9th POSSESSION — Make Your Layups
    10th POSSESSION — Make Your Free Throws

    GAME CHANGING PLAY — Triple Threat Position

2nd Quarter – Preparation & Process

    1st POSSESSION — Build Muscle Memory
    2nd POSSESSION — Practice is Harder Than the Game
    3rd POSSESSION — How You Practice Is How You Play
    4th POSSESSION — Start Close and Work Your Way Out
    5th POSSESSION — Proper Spacing
    6th POSSESSION — Counter Moves
    7th POSSESSION — Stay Ready
    8th POSSESSION — Don't Let the Clock Rush You
    9th POSSESSION — Rest Properly
    10th POSSESSION — Study The Film

    GAME CHANGING PLAY — Handling Crowd Noise

HALFTIME
SPECIAL PRESENTATION
Ode To The Ball

3rd Quarter – Effort, Energy & Pace

    1st POSSESSION — Have a Motor
    2nd POSSESSION — Play With Pace and Tempo
    3rd POSSESSION — Run The Floor
    4th POSSESSION — Dive on Loose Balls
    5th POSSESSION — Cut to Score
    6th POSSESSION — Get Back on D!
    7th POSSESSION — Take a Charge
    8th POSSESSION — Extending a Hand
    9th POSSESSION — Help and Recover
    10th POSSESSION — Three Man Weave

    GAME CHANGING PLAY —Move Without The Ball

4th Quarter – Awareness & Wisdom

    1st POSSESSION — Stop the Ball
    2nd POSSESSION — A Bad Shot Is Better Than a Turnover
    3rd POSSESSION — Situational Awareness
    4th POSSESSION — Touch Every Line
    5th POSSESSION — Protect the House
    6th POSSESSION — Finish the Play
    7th POSSESSION — Who Got Next?
    8th POSSESSION — Call the Lineup
    9th POSSESSION — Make It, Take It
    10th POSSESSION — Take Over the Game

    GAME CHANGING PLAY — Chip Away

GAME WINNING FREE THROWS— 2 shots

FINAL BUZZER — It Was A Good Run

POST GAME SPEECH — Cherish the Moments

GRAB YOUR BAG. LET'S GET OUTTA HERE — A Letter to The Game

The Coach's Office

Before the lessons on these pages were ever taught, they were first modeled, corrected, and reinforced by coaches who cared enough to demand more. What I learned about the game of basketball, and about life, was shaped by men who saw potential, spoke truth, and held me to a standard worth reaching.

Coach Darrell Halloran
Head Coach - Pace University

Coach Halloran believed in me when the big-name, big-school coaches overlooked me. My basketball IQ skyrocketed under him. However, it was our final conversation after my senior season that was most meaningful. He told me it had been an honor to coach me, and what he said next gives me chills to this very day. He said "Layne Fields you are going to be a great dad someday". I made it my life's mission to fulfill those words.

John "Coach B" Byrne
Assistant Coach - Pace University

Coach B was the assistant responsible for the details. He ran the skills and drills that focused on the small, often unnoticed aspects of the game that never show up in the box score. Without his influence, several of the concepts in this book would have gone unrealized. He is one of those unspoken treasures in the life of a developing young man, and my appreciation for him is immense.

Coach Steve Paskiewicz

Head Coach - Riverhead High School

Coach Steve Paskiewicz was my varsity coach during my senior year of high school. He gave me the freedom to be creative, to lead, and to shine. Beyond the court, he treated me like a son and was present for several of the most meaningful moments of my life. My respect and admiration for him are beyond words. Most importantly, he was a brother in Christ, and I loved him.

Coach Wayne Rana

Head Coach - Riverhead High School

Coach Wayne Rana was my first varsity basketball coach. He believed in me enough to bench a twelfth-grade starter and put me in the lineup as a sophomore. He taught me to compete with confidence even as an underclassman. That belief continued when he named me co-captain as a junior, strengthening my confidence as a leader.

Coach Charles Van Slyke

Former Head Coach - Riverhead High School

Coach Van Slyke retired before I reached high school, but he remained a teacher at the school and an encourager in my life. He saw enough potential in me to pay my way to basketball camp when I was in the tenth grade when my mom couldn't afford it. Even though I didn't play for him, he constantly encouraged me to keep my grades up, work on my game, and to be fundamentally sound.

Coach Willie Patterson

Former Coach - Riverhead High School

Coach Willie Patterson was the first coach to instill discipline and excellence in my game and in my life. I watched him closely, both on and off the court because he was my science teacher. He modeled how a man should carry himself. How preparation, appearance, and conduct all matter. He is the reason I wear nice suits, neckties, and polished shoes. More importantly, he taught me dignity and respect alongside the game of basketball.

Coach Ben Gamble

Player/Asst. Coach - St. Anthony High School of Jersey City
Current Head Coach- Bayonne (NJ) High School

Ben was my freshman year roommate and point guard. He's the first player that I ever saw cry after a loss, and I didn't understand the tears. He was a 2x New Jersey state champ and 3x county champ. Losing was foreign to him. Winning was foreign to me. That year Ben took me under his wing and began teaching me how to win. I knew then that he'd be a great coach someday. I thought I loved basketball. Until I met Ben.

Unfortunately, Ben cried 20 more times that season....

However, as of this writing, he's working on a legendary career as a High School coach in New Jersey. It wouldn't shock me if one day he's in the state Hall of Fame alongside his mentor, Coach Bob Hurley, Sr.

Starting Lineup

The Ball Is the Star

Before there were shoe deals, highlight reels, social media followers, and debate shows arguing over greatness, there was the ball. Before arenas, scoreboards, and million-dollar contracts, there was a simple idea. Put said ball through the peach basket hanging on a pole.

Dr. James Naismith did not design a game to glorify players. He designed a game to teach cooperation, movement, and discipline. From the very beginning, the game was never about who you were. It was about what you did with what you were given.

The basketball itself was, is, and always will be the star of the game.

That's why players want to touch it. They need to feel it. That's why they fight for possession. It's why they try to keep it from going out of bounds. It's the reason they dive on it when it's loose. And ultimately, it's what everyone came to see. They came to see what happened with the ball.

People don't really show up to watch personalities. They show up to watch the ball go through the rim. It's the ball that scores. The player is just the instrument used to creatively make it happen. And there have been many who make it rather entertaining to watch.

However, players come and go. Jerseys change. Eras rise and fall. But the ball remains. It is constant. It is impartial. It rewards discipline and exposes carelessness. It responds honestly to how it is handled. You can't fake your way with it for long.

The ball tells the truth. Ball don't lie!

When I was young, I didn't understand that. Like most young players, I wanted the spotlight. I wanted the notoriety. I wanted the applause that came from making plays and being recognized. The ball gave me those things, and I enjoyed them. But over time, the ball began teaching me something deeper.

No matter how good I thought I was, the ball never belonged to me. I was just it's steward for a season. I was entrusted with it for moments at a time. My job was not to dominate it, but to handle it well. To protect it. To advance it. To share it. To respect it.

That lesson didn't stop on the court. Life works the same way.

Opportunities are entrusted, not owned. Influence is borrowed. Time is limited. Responsibility is temporary. What you do with what you're given matters more than how long you get to hold it.

The ball does not care about your résumé. It does not respond to entitlement. It does not bend to ego. It responds to preparation, discipline, awareness, and humility. Handle it well, and it will reward you. Treat it carelessly, and it will expose you.

That's why humility is the best posture for a great life.

No matter how skilled you become, you are not the point. No matter how much attention you receive, you are not the center. The responsibility endures even when the spotlight fades. Long after the cheers die down, the question remains the same: What did you do with what was entrusted to you?

This book is not about glorifying players. It's about honoring the lessons. It's about recognizing that while players are celebrated, the ball itself is still the sacred trust. Handle it well.

Jump Ball

The Sound That Changed Everything!

I fell in love with basketball as a 13-year-old eighth grader in 1979.

Baseball was my first love. I was a very good baseball player as a kid. I was a star in my local Little League, and most people thought I was going to do something special with that game. Perhaps the big leagues.

Baseball felt natural to me. Comfortable. Familiar. Basketball was just a fun time with my friends. Until the 8th grade I had never played organized basketball.

Then one night in 1979, something happened.

I was watching the NCAA Championship game featuring Magic Johnson and Larry Bird. I could not take my eyes off the screen. Larry Bird was unlike anyone I had ever seen. He was not flashy, but he was surgical. Confident. Ruthless in the quietest way. And then there was Magic! That smile. That joy. That flair. He played the game like he owned it and loved it at the same time.

Something clicked in me that night.

Magic immediately became my sports idol and from that moment on, basketball dominated my thoughts. It was all I could think about. All I wanted to do. I carried a basketball with me everywhere I went. I slept with it nearby.

As I grew a little taller, the game started to open up for me. The floor made more sense. The angels. The timing. The strategy. I was dialed in.

I loved everything about it. Athleticism. The competition. The recognition that came with being halfway decent. The attention from peers. Friday night games in New York. The energy in the gym.

But more than anything else, I fell in love with the sound. The sound of sneakers squeaking on the hardwood. That sound was music to my ears.

If I pulled up to a gym and heard sneakers squeaking while I was getting out of the car, my heart would start racing. I felt like I was missing out. I could not get inside fast enough.

The louder the squeak, the more intense the game. More squeaks meant harder play, stiffer competition, and real effort.

Squeaky sneakers meant people were competing. That sound meant people were playing hard and putting in some work. Playing pick-up like it was game 7 of the NBA Finals. Playing for keeps!

That sound meant the game mattered. Guts and glory. Testosterone and trash talk. Bragging rights and hierarchy being established. For me, squeaky sneakers meant somebody in there was hoopin'!

That sound is still music to my ears. Basketball's beat became the soundtrack of my life. If my sneakers weren't squeaking, then I wasn't breathing. I had to have it. I needed it.

As the years went on, I realized something important. Basketball was teaching me far more than how to play a game. It was shaping how I thought, how I responded to pressure, how I handled success and failure, how I related to teammates, and how I carried myself in life.

The gym became a classroom. The hardwood became a teacher. The game became a guide.

This book is a collection of those lessons.

It is for anyone who grew up in a 4,700 square foot rectangle with hash marks and stripes. For anyone who stayed late to get shots up. For anyone who touched all the lines when nobody was watching. For anyone who learned about discipline, humility, leadership, and resilience with every drop of sweat that bounced off the floor.

Basketball gave me language for life. It gave me perspective. It gave me principles. And it gave me a soundtrack.

Squeaky sneakers.

Because ball really is life.

Foundation & Character

1st POSSESSION

Be Available

Basketball Theory

The first ability is availability. Coaches can't play you if you're not there. You can't improve if you don't show up. Progress requires presence. Great players make themselves available to learn, to practice, to be coached, and to compete—even when they're tired, discouraged, or dealing with less-than-ideal conditions.

Life Application

Show up. Be present. Even when you don't feel like it. Even when the circumstances aren't perfect. Growth happens through consistency, not convenience. If you make yourself available to learn and grow, not only will your skills improve, but your life will, too. People are far more willing to invest in those who reliably show up.

Hardwood Insight

Coaches trust the players they can count on. Availability builds trust long before talent takes over. A dependable player will always have an opportunity to earn minutes.

Real-Life Parallel

Opportunities often come disguised as ordinary days that require faithfulness. Miss enough days, and doors quietly close. Stay present, and doors begin to open without you forcing them.

Leadership Insight

Leaders are visible. They are present. They don't disappear when things get uncomfortable. Availability communicates commitment, stability, and reliability to everyone watching.

The Squeak

Show up. You will be glad you did. Growth rarely happens in dramatic leaps. It happens through consistent presence. Showing up builds rhythm, trust, and opportunity. Even on days when energy is low or motivation is thin, presence creates momentum. Many breakthroughs are missed not because of lack of ability, but because of absence. Being there positions you for moments you cannot plan but must be present to receive.

The Next Play

Where have you been inconsistent lately, showing up some days but disappearing on others?
What would change if you committed to being present, not just physically, but mentally and emotionally as well?
Decide to show up fully. Stay available. Watch what begins to open simply because you were there.

2nd POSSESSION

Listen to The Coach

Basketball Theory

One of the first lessons every player learns is simple. Listen to the coach. Before you learn plays, before you learn strategy, before you learn how to read defenses, you learn to listen. Coaches see the floor differently. They have perspectives you do not yet have. They know what is coming before you feel it.

Players who listen learn faster. Players who resist instruction stay stuck. Talent may get you noticed, but coachability determines how far you go. Every great player, without exception, submitted to instruction before they were allowed to lead.

Life Application

Life works the same way. Be coachable. Submit to authority. Learn to listen to parents, elders, mentors, and leaders who have walked the road before you. Obedience and respect are not weaknesses. They are disciplines that build wisdom. You do not know everything. None of us do. Growth begins when humility replaces resistance.

Hardwood Insight

Every coach can spot it immediately. One player nods, adjusts, and applies instruction. Another rolls their eyes, argues, or pretends to listen while continuing to do their own thing. The difference shows up quickly. The first player improves. The second player plateaus. Listening does not mean blind agreement. It means teachability. It means recognizing that correction is not an attack, but an investment. Coaches correct players they believe in. The same posture determines growth far beyond the court.

Real-Life Parallel

Many people struggle not because they lack opportunity, but because they resist instruction. They reject correction. They bristle at authority. They confuse independence with wisdom. But the people who grow fastest are the ones willing to learn. They listen. They apply. They adjust. Over time, those same people become trusted voices, sought-after leaders, and steady influences. Growth favors the teachable.

Leadership Insight

Strong leaders were once strong followers. They learned when to speak and when to listen. They respected authority before they were given authority. They submitted to structure before they were trusted with responsibility. Leadership that bypasses humility eventually collapses under its own weight. Those who refuse to be coached rarely develop the capacity to coach others well.

The Squeak

Coachability is character. It reveals humility, maturity, and self-awareness. A teachable posture keeps you growing long after talent levels off. When you remain coachable, you signal that growth matters more than ego and progress matters more than pride.

The Next Play

Who is speaking into your life right now that you may not be fully listening to?
Where have you dismissed instruction because it challenged your comfort or confidence?
Lower your guard. Open your ears. Apply what you are being taught. Listening today prepares you to lead tomorrow.

3rd POSSESSION

Discipline Over Talent

Basketball Theory

Talent gets noticed early, but discipline determines who lasts. The game is full of gifted players who never reached their potential—not because they lacked ability, but because they lacked discipline. Meanwhile, others with less natural talent became legends because discipline sharpened what they had. Michael Jordan. Kobe Bryant. Their greatness wasn't accidental. It was cultivated through relentless discipline. Sure, they were immensely talented, but it was their discipline that made them legendary.

Talent opens doors. Discipline keeps you in the room.

Life Application:

A disciplined life is one of the primary keys to long-term prosperity and excellence. Discipline governs how you manage your time, your body, your money, your relationships, and your responsibilities. Without it, talent becomes a liability instead of an asset.

Hardwood Insight

Most coaches would prefer a very good, but disciplined player over an undisciplined but talented one any day. Disciplined players show up early. They listen. They run the drill the right way, even when nobody is watching. They do not need constant motivation because their habits do the heavy lifting. Talent is exciting, but discipline is dependable. When the season gets long, the legs get tired, and the pressure gets heavy, discipline is what shows up when motivation fades.

Real-Life Parallel

Life does not reward potential. It rewards patterns. Plenty of people are gifted but inconsistent. They rely on spurts of effort instead of systems, bursts of energy instead of habits. Over time, that approach collapses under its own weight. Discipline turns good intentions into repeatable behavior. It becomes the bridge between who you are today and who you are trying to become tomorrow.

Leadership Insight

Disciplined leaders create stability. They keep commitments. They manage emotions. They maintain standards even when it is inconvenient or uncomfortable. Undisciplined leaders burn bridges, create chaos, and undermine their own influence. Discipline is not restrictive. It is protective. It guards credibility, preserves trust, and sustains leadership over time.

The Squeak

Talent makes noise. Discipline makes history. Talent may open doors, but discipline keeps them open. Discipline outlasts excitement, survives adversity, and carries you through seasons when enthusiasm alone is not enough.

The Next Play

Where does your life need more discipline right now, not tomorrow or someday, but today?
What habit, routine, or standard needs to be established or reinforced?
Do not wait to feel motivated. Build the habit and let discipline carry you forward.

4th POSSESSION

Fundamentals Before Flash

Basketball Theory

Every great player, no matter how gifted, is built on fundamentals. Shooting form. Footwork. Passing. Defense. Ball handling. These aren't glamorous, but they are essential. Coaches drill them relentlessly because when the pressure rises, you don't rise to the occasion—you fall back on your fundamentals.

Flash may get attention, but fundamentals win games. Miss the basics, and everything else breaks down.

Life Application

Basic life skills and ongoing personal development build a great life. Character, discipline, communication, work ethic, and consistency aren't optional. They are the foundation. Skip them, and no amount of talent or opportunity will save you.

Hardwood Insight

Young players love highlights.
Veteran players love efficiency.

The older you get around the game, the more you appreciate the little things done well. A crisp pass. Proper spacing. Solid defense. The stuff that doesn't make the crowd roar—but makes the coach trust you.

When games get tight, coaches don't call fancy plays. They call simple ones and trust players to execute the basics under pressure.

Life is no different.

Real-Life Parallel

People often want shortcuts in life. They want success without discipline. Results without preparation. Respect without responsibility. But fundamentals do not bend for anyone. They are impartial, patient, and persistent. If you do not know how to manage money, more money will not help. If you cannot communicate clearly, more influence will not fix it. If you lack integrity, more opportunity will only expose what is already there. Growth does not skip steps. It builds on basics that are practiced, not admired.

Leadership Insight

Strong leaders obsess over fundamentals. They never assume the basics are beneath them. They revisit them regularly, reinforce them intentionally, and model them consistently. Leaders often fail not because they lacked knowledge, vision, or ideas, but because they neglected what they already knew. Mastery is rarely about learning something new. More often, it is about returning to what works and doing it well.

The Squeak

Fundamentals are not flashy, but they are faithful. They show up every day, hold things together under pressure, and carry weight when conditions are not ideal. When everything else breaks down, fundamentals remain. They are the quiet strength behind every sustainable success.

The Next Play

What basic area of your life needs renewed attention right now?
Where have you drifted from what you know works because it stopped feeling exciting?
Get back to the fundamentals, because everything strong starts there.

5th POSSESSION

Protect the Ball

Basketball Theory

Protecting the ball is non-negotiable. Turnovers cost possessions, momentum, and games. Coaches teach players to keep the ball high, use strong hands, pivot with purpose, and value every touch. You don't win by making spectacular plays if you're careless with the ball. The fastest way to the bench is showing you can't be trusted to protect what's in your hands.

Life Application

Steward your resources. Time, money, relationships, reputation, health, and opportunity are all entrusted to you. Carelessness creates loss. Discipline preserves what matters. If you don't protect what you've been given, life will eventually take it out of your hands.

Hardwood Insight

Coaches don't yell "be flashy." They yell "be strong with the ball." You can miss a shot and stay on the floor. You can't keep turning it over and expect more chances.

Real-Life Parallel

Many people don't fail because they lack opportunity. They fail because they mishandled what they already had. Broken trust, wasted time, poor financial decisions, and neglected health all start with not protecting the ball.

Leadership Insight

Leaders who protect resources earn trust. Leaders who are careless create instability. Stewardship is one of the clearest indicators of maturity and readiness for greater responsibility. How a leader handles time, people, finances, influence, and opportunity reveals their true capacity. Trust grows when others see that what is entrusted to you is handled with care, discipline, and foresight. Neglect signals immaturity. Protection signals readiness.

The Squeak

Value every possession. Nothing meaningful is accidental. Every possession carries potential, and every careless moment carries risk. In basketball, possession determines opportunity. In life and leadership, it determines outcomes. When you value what you have, you slow down, stay aware, and act with intention. Possessions are not unlimited. How you treat them reveals what you truly value.

The Next Play

What area of your life needs better protection right now because it has been handled too casually or taken for granted?
What would change if you tightened your grip, raised your standard, and handled it with intention?
This possession matters. Treat it like it does.

6th POSSESSION

No Compound Mistakes

Basketball Theory

Do not make compound mistakes. One mistake is understandable. Two in a row is avoidable. Miss a shot? Get back on defense. Turn the ball over? Do not follow it up with a foul or an argument.

Compound mistakes turn small problems into big ones. They usually happen when emotion overrides discipline. Smart players limit damage by stabilizing after error instead of reacting impulsively.

Life Application

Life works the same way. One poor decision does not require another. Failure does not justify recklessness. Discipline after failure is a mark of maturity. You cannot always avoid making mistakes, but you can always avoid compounding them. Wisdom shows up in what you do *after* something goes wrong. Recovery begins the moment you refuse to add damage.

Hardwood Insight

Most breakdowns are not caused by the first mistake. They are caused by the reaction to it. The frustration foul. The rushed decision. The emotional response. Veteran players understand this. They slow the moment down. They protect the possession. They stop the bleeding. That discipline separates experience from impulse, and it transfers cleanly to life.

Real-Life Parallel

Many people dig deeper holes by reacting poorly. A bad day leads to bad choices. A tough conversation leads to avoidance. A failure leads to quitting. Momentum swings not because of the mistake itself, but because of what follows it. Discipline is what stops the slide. You regain control by refusing to add damage when things are already difficult.

Leadership Insight

Effective leaders manage moments, not just outcomes. They correct mistakes calmly. They stabilize environments quickly. They prevent one error from becoming a crisis. Leadership often shows up most clearly after something goes wrong. How a leader responds in those moments determines whether trust erodes or strengthens.

The Squeak

One mistake is human. Two in a row is a choice. Discipline is the difference between a setback and a collapse. The ability to pause, regain control, and respond wisely keeps one misstep from defining the entire possession.

The Next Play

Where do you need to stop a mistake from becoming something bigger right now?
What would change if you slowed the moment down and chose discipline instead of reaction?
Protect the possession. Stop the bleeding.

7ᵗʰ POSSESSION

Have a Short Memory

Basketball Theory

Great players develop a short memory. Missed shots happen. Bad passes happen. Defensive breakdowns happen. The players who last do not dwell on the last play. They reset immediately and focus on the next possession.

If you carry one mistake into the next play, it multiplies the damage. Basketball moves too fast for regret. The game rewards those who can acknowledge a mistake, learn from it, and move on without emotional residue.

Life Application

Life requires the same discipline. You will make mistakes. You will say the wrong thing. You will fail at times. A short memory allows you to recover quickly and re-engage with clarity instead of shame or frustration.

Owning a mistake does not require living in it. Learn, reset, and move forward.

Hardwood Insight

Coaches talk about this constantly. You miss a shot. Get back on defense. You turn the ball over. Sprint back. You get beat. Recover and help. The game does not pause for frustration or regret. Players who sulk become liabilities because they stay mentally stuck in the last moment. Players who reset become trustworthy because they stay engaged in the current one. Emotional control is not suppression. It is maturity. The ability to reset quickly keeps you useful to the team.

Real-Life Parallel

Many people stay stuck longer than necessary because they keep replaying what already happened. They rehearse failure. They relive embarrassment. They punish themselves far beyond the lesson that needed to be learned. A short memory frees you to stay present. Growth requires attention to what is next, not fixation on what is past. You cannot move forward while staring backward.

Leadership Insight

Strong leaders reset quickly. They do not spiral after setbacks or lead from a wounded emotional state. They acknowledge failure honestly without allowing it to dictate direction. A leader's ability to reset sets the emotional temperature for everyone else. When leaders move on with clarity and composure, teams regain confidence and momentum.

The Squeak

Next play. Good or bad, move on. Carrying yesterday's mistake into today's moment only compounds damage. Resetting is not denial. It is discipline. The ability to let go and re-engage keeps you effective and dependable.

The Next Play

What mistake are you still carrying that should have been released already?
What would change if you learned the lesson without reliving the pain?
Reset your focus. Move forward with clarity. Play the next play.

8th POSSESSION

Play Inside Out

Basketball Theory

Offense is best played inside out. You get the ball into the paint either by dribble penetration or by pass. When the ball goes into the paint, the defense must collapse to stop the most immediate threat, which is a shot at the rim. Defenders leave their assignments and converge on the ball.

Once the defense collapses, options open up. You can finish at the basket yourself. You can pass to a teammate cutting to the rim. Or you can kick the ball out to a wide open shooter on the perimeter. He is open because the defense followed the ball into the paint.

Good offense does not force options. It creates them.

Life Application

Play life from the inside out. Get right with God. Live a high moral existence. Be a person of deep integrity and abiding character. When your inner life is ordered properly, life presents more options. Decisions become clearer. Pressure becomes manageable. Confusion gives way to clarity.

Hardwood Insight

Great teams do not drift around the perimeter hoping something opens up. They attack the heart of the defense with intention. They establish position. They create advantage. Then they make the best decision available.

When a team refuses to go inside, the offense stagnates. Shots become forced. Timing breaks down. Everything feels rushed.

The same thing happens in life when your inner world is neglected.

Real-Life Parallel

When your inner life is disordered, everything feels limited.

You feel boxed in.
You feel reactive.
You feel like every decision is a bad option.

But when your values are clear and your character is solid, pressure produces options instead of panic. You are not scrambling for answers because your foundation is already set.

Inside alignment produces outside freedom.

Leadership Insight

Strong leaders lead from the inside out.

They do not sacrifice integrity for influence.
They do not compromise character for convenience.
They do not build success on unstable foundations.

When leaders are grounded internally, they can see the floor clearly and make wise decisions under pressure.

The Squeak

Get to the paint. Take a real, hard, close look at yourself and make an honest assessment. Then begin the work of self-improvement and see all the options that life presents.

The Next Play

Where does your inner life need attention right now?

Start on the inside. Order your heart. Live with integrity. The options you are looking for will come into view.

9ᵗʰ POSSESSION

Make Your Layups

Basketball Theory

Layups are theoretically the easiest shot in the game. They are close, high-percentage, and often uncontested when executed properly. Coaches expect players to convert layups because missing them wastes effort and momentum. Great teams do not beat themselves by failing to finish the simplest opportunities.

Life Application

There are basic responsibilities in life that you simply have to handle. Show up. Do the work. Pay attention. Take care of what's right in front of you. Neglecting simple tasks creates unnecessary difficulty and forces you to work harder than you should.

Hardwood Insight

Nothing frustrates a coach faster than a missed layup. Not because the player lacks talent, but because the moment did not require talent. It required focus, awareness, and execution. Layups are about attention to detail. They are the simplest shots in the game, yet they often expose complacency, distraction, or lack of discipline. Missed layups shift momentum, deflate teams, and create unnecessary pressure that never should have existed.

Real-Life Parallel

Many people chase big wins while ignoring small responsibilities. They want promotion but will not manage their time. They want influence but will not keep commitments. They want opportunity but neglect preparation. Miss enough layups in life and you spend your energy recovering instead of progressing. Small neglect compounds quickly and quietly becomes a pattern.

Leadership Insight

Strong leaders handle the basics consistently. They return calls. They show up on time. They follow through. That reliability builds trust long before vision or charisma ever do. When people know you can be counted on for the simple things, they trust you with bigger responsibilities. Leaders earn difficult assignments by proving they can execute the easy ones without supervision.

The Squeak

Finish the easy ones. The layup is the most basic responsibility in the game, yet it reveals focus more than talent ever will. Nobody celebrates it, but everyone remembers when it is missed. Making the easy ones is about discipline, presence, and respect for the moment. Players who finish layups show they are locked in, dependable, and serious about winning. In life and leadership, the same rule applies. When you consistently handle what requires the least effort but the most care, you build credibility. Teams trust players who do not waste simple opportunities. Leaders trust people who do not need reminders to do what should already be done.

The Next Play

What basic responsibility have you been overlooking because it feels too small to matter?
What would change if you treated it with the same seriousness as a big opportunity?
Handle it today.
Make the layup that is already in front of you.

10th POSSESSION

Make Your Free Throws

Basketball Theory

Free throws are uncontested opportunities for free points. No defense. No screen. No excuse. Coaches expect players to convert because free throws often decide close games. They reward preparation, routine, and mental discipline more than athleticism.

Life Application

Life presents windows of opportunity that must be recognized and acted on before they close. Some opportunities are uncontested. They require decisiveness, confidence, and follow-through. Hesitation, distraction, or fear can cost you points you'll never get back.

Hardwood Insight

Free throws expose fundamentals. When legs are tired and pressure is high, mechanics and routine either hold up or break down. The work you did before the game shows up at the line.

Real-Life Parallel

There are moments in life when the path is clear. A job opening. A conversation that needs to happen. An opportunity to step forward. Nobody is stopping you but you. When those moments come, you have to take the shot.

Leadership Insight

Strong leaders recognize time-bound opportunities and act decisively. They understand that not every opportunity lingers and not every window stays open. Preparation creates confidence, and confidence fuels action. Leaders who hesitate waiting for perfect conditions often miss moments that required courage, not certainty. When the window opens, decisive leaders trust their work, step forward, and live with the result.

The Squeak

Free points matter. In basketball, free throws are uncontested opportunities to score, yet they still require focus, discipline, and belief. Nobody guards you. Nobody rushes you. The only thing that can stop you is hesitation or lack of confidence in your preparation. Players who value free points understand momentum. They know games are often decided by what should have been easy.

In life and leadership, free points show up as clear opportunities, open doors, and moments where resistance is low but decisiveness is required. Ignoring those moments is careless. Failing to act because of fear or doubt wastes opportunities that may never return. Wise leaders take free points seriously because they understand that small, uncontested wins often determine larger outcomes.

The Next Play

What opportunity is in front of you right now that will not be there forever?
Where do preparation and opportunity intersect in this season of your life?
Step up. Trust your work. Take the shot with confidence while the line is still clear.

GAME CHANGING PLAY

Be a Triple Threat

In basketball, the triple threat position is simple, but it's not casual. When a player catches the ball and squares up, they immediately become a threat to pass, shoot, or drive. Nothing has happened yet, but everything is possible. The defender has to respect all three options. They can't relax. They can't assume. The game changes the moment a player is prepared.

A player in triple threat is always considered a threat to score or to make a play that leads to a score. That's what forces the defense to react. If opponents don't recognize you as a threat, they don't guard you. They sag off. They help elsewhere. And suddenly, the game shifts. In essence, you're playing four against five, putting your team at an immediate disadvantage. Readiness isn't personal. It affects everyone on the floor.

The triple threat isn't about making a move. It's about being ready to make any move. That readiness changes how you're perceived. Teammates trust you. Defenders hesitate. Coaches notice. The player in triple threat doesn't rush. They don't panic. They don't waste motion. They are balanced, aware, and intentional. The power of the position is not what you do with the ball, but what the defense has to consider because of the posture you've taken.

Life works the same way.

In life, you are called to be a contributor, not a bystander. When you fail to develop your skills, your discipline, or your character, people stop expecting much from you. Just like on the court, when others don't see you as a threat, they don't take you seriously. Opportunities shrink. Responsibility shifts elsewhere. And the people connected to you are forced to carry more than they should. Unprepared living doesn't just limit you. It puts others at a disadvantage.

Being a triple threat in life means you bring value wherever you go. You can contribute ideas, effort, wisdom, and action. You're capable of creating progress or helping someone else succeed. You don't have to be the star, but you must be a threat to make something happen. That kind of readiness earns trust, expands opportunity, and keeps you in the flow of meaningful work.

The danger is in showing up unprepared and hoping something works out. Defenders can smell hesitation. Life does the same. When you lack preparation, pressure exposes you. You rush. You force decisions. You settle for bad shots because you don't trust your handle, your vision, or your footing. That's true on the court, and it's true in life.

The triple threat is a reminder that you don't rise to the moment. You fall back on your preparation.

When you live in a triple threat posture, you don't need to rush the game. You let the game come to you. You see the floor. You read the moment. You make the right decision, not the fastest one. And over time, people stop overlooking you. Doubters reconsider. Opponents rethink. Not because you said anything, but because your readiness speaks for you.

That's a game changer.

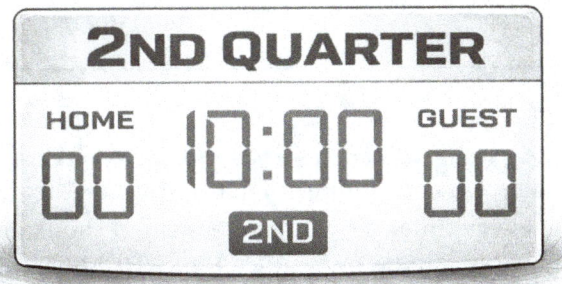

Preparation & Process

1st POSSESSION

Build Muscle Memory

Basketball Theory

Repetition builds muscle memory. That's why free throw routines stay the same every time. It's why players shoot thousands of shots from the same spots on the floor. It's why we dribble and pound the rock with our off hand until our joints ache. Muscle memory allows the body to respond correctly without conscious thought. When pressure rises, the body defaults to what it has repeated most.

Life Application

Life works the same way. Routines build rhythm. Rhythm builds memory. Memory builds habits. Habits shape outcomes. That's why we make our bed every day. That's why we rehearse sales presentations, speeches, conversations, and decisions before they matter. Repetition turns preparation into instinct, and instinct makes life manageable under pressure.

Hardwood Insight

When the game is tight, players do not suddenly rise to a new level. They fall back on their training. Under pressure, mechanics reveal habits. Muscle memory takes over when emotions are high, legs are tired, and decisions must be made quickly. Players who have put in disciplined, intentional reps continue to execute cleanly. Players who have relied on shortcuts, inconsistency, or raw talent alone begin to unravel. Pressure does not create skill. It exposes what has already been rehearsed.

Real-Life Parallel

Life works the same way. When stress hits, you do not suddenly become disciplined. You revert to whatever you have practiced. If your routines are sloppy, your responses will be sloppy. If your routines are intentional, your responses will be steady. Crisis does not introduce new behavior. It reveals existing patterns. The way you handle pressure is a reflection of what you repeat when no one is watching.

Leadership Insight

Strong leaders build personal routines before expecting performance from others. They understand that consistency in private produces credibility in public. Leaders who lack structure struggle to lead with clarity under pressure. Leaders who have disciplined rhythms bring calm, direction, and stability when situations intensify. Before leaders ask others to execute, they make sure their own habits are sound.

The Squeak

Repetition wins. Talent may flash, emotion may surge, and motivation may spike, but repetition endures. The work you repeat becomes the response you rely on. Repetition turns discipline into instinct and preparation into confidence. When the moment gets loud, fast, and heavy, you will not think your way through it. You will play your habits. That is why repetition matters more than intention.

The Next Play

What daily routine are you repeating right now that is quietly shaping your future?
Which habits are strengthening you under pressure, and which ones are setting you up to fold?
Strengthen the routines that serve you. Eliminate the ones that do not. Repetition is already deciding the outcome.

2nd POSSESSION

Practice Should Be Harder Than the Game

Basketball Theory

Practice is designed to stretch you beyond comfort. Coaches push pace, demand precision, and correct mistakes because the goal of practice is not ease. It is readiness. When practice is harder than the game, the game slows down mentally. Movements feel familiar. Decisions feel clearer. You have already experienced the stress, the speed, and the fatigue in preparation, so the moment does not shock you. Hard practice removes surprise.

Life Application

Life rewards those who prepare deeply. Casual preparation creates fragile confidence. When pressure shows up, it overwhelms people who have only trained in comfort. Hard preparation creates calm execution. When you have already done the work, the moment does not feel foreign or intimidating. Preparation turns pressure into recognition instead of panic.

Hardwood Insight

Players who panic in games usually trained in comfort. They avoided intensity, resisted correction, and relied on talent to carry them. Players who stay calm trained under stress. They were pushed, corrected, and tested long before the lights came on. The difference shows up immediately when the game tightens.

Real-Life Parallel

Big moments rarely announce themselves. Interviews, emergencies, leadership opportunities, and crises arrive suddenly. There is no warm-up. No pause button. Preparation determines whether you freeze or function. When the moment arrives, you do not rise to it. You reveal what you trained for.

Leadership Insight

Strong leaders raise standards before the spotlight arrives. They do not wait until the moment to demand excellence. They create environments where pressure is familiar, accountability is normal, and expectations are clear. Leaders who train people under pressure prepare them to perform when it matters most.

The Squeak

Train under pressure until pressure is no longer stressful. Comfort is a liar. It whispers that you are ready when you are not. Stress in preparation builds confidence in performance. When difficulty becomes familiar, fear loses its grip. The goal is not to eliminate pressure, but to master it through disciplined preparation.

The Next Play

Where are you preparing at a level that is too comfortable right now? What standard needs to be raised before the moment arrives? Increase the difficulty today so pressure does not overwhelm you tomorrow.

3rd POSSESSION

How You Practice Is How You Play

Basketball Theory

Players carry practice habits into games. There is no separation. If you jog through drills, you will jog through possessions. If you cut corners in practice, you will cut corners under pressure. Habits do not disappear when the lights come on. They surface. Practice is not rehearsal for perfection. It is conditioning for response. What you repeat when it "doesn't matter" becomes automatic when it suddenly does.

Life Application

Life works the same way. How you handle daily responsibilities is how you will handle major opportunities. Your habits are rehearsals for your future. Ordinary days quietly shape extraordinary moments. If you want different outcomes, you cannot rely on hope or motivation. You must practice differently in the ordinary. Small disciplines compound into big results over time.

Hardwood Insight

You do not rise to the occasion. You default to your habits. Under pressure, there is no time to invent discipline. You execute what you have trained. The game exposes preparation, not intention.

Real-Life Parallel

Many people want breakthroughs without building patterns. They look for moments to change their lives instead of habits that shape them. But consistency is what creates trust, confidence, and credibility over time. What you do repeatedly becomes what people expect from you, including yourself.

Leadership Insight

Strong leaders model discipline long before they demand it from others. They understand that culture is not created by speeches, but by behavior. What you tolerate in yourself eventually becomes the standard around you. Leaders who lack discipline cannot produce disciplined teams. Personal habits always lead public outcomes.

The Squeak

Practice with purpose. Every rep is a vote for who you are becoming. Purposeful practice sharpens focus, reinforces standards, and builds trust in yourself. When you treat preparation casually, you train inconsistency. When you practice with intention, you train reliability. Purpose in practice turns effort into identity.

The Next Play

What habit are you rehearsing daily that is shaping your future, for better or for worse?
Where do you need to raise your standard in the ordinary so you are ready for the extraordinary?
Practice with purpose. Your habits are already writing the next chapter.

4th POSSESSION

Start Close and Work Your Way Out

Basketball Theory

Great shooters begin close to the basket. Form shots. Layups. Free throws. Rhythm comes before range. Confidence is built near the rim before it is tested at distance. Coaches do not start players behind the arc because distance magnifies flaws. Close-range work builds mechanics, balance, touch, and trust. When the foundation is sound, range becomes an extension, not a gamble. Skipping steps produces forced shots and fragile confidence.

Life Application

Life rewards the same progression. Start small and grow methodically and steadily. Small wins compound. Foundational disciplines create long-term strength. Do not despise early stages or modest beginnings. They are building mechanics you will rely on later. When pressure increases, you fall back on what was built early. Solid foundations make growth sustainable.

Hardwood Insight

Players who skip fundamentals look rushed and inconsistent. Their movements lack rhythm because their base is unstable. Players who master the basics look smooth, balanced, and confident. The game slows down for them because their foundation does not crack under pressure.

Real-Life Parallel

Many people want big platforms without building a base. They want influence without discipline, visibility without preparation, and responsibility without reliability. Growth requires patience and progression. Skipping steps may produce short-term attention, but it rarely produces long-term success.

Leadership Insight

Wise leaders respect process. They do not rush people into positions they are not prepared to carry. They understand that promotion without preparation creates pressure, failure, and burnout. Leaders who build patiently develop people who can sustain responsibility when the stage gets bigger.

The Squeak

Build the base first. Everything strong is built from the ground up. The unseen work close to the basket determines what happens when you step back and shoot from distance. When fundamentals are solid, confidence is earned, not forced. Strong bases create smooth execution and steady growth over time.

The Next Play

What basic discipline do you need to master before expanding further?
Where have you tried to stretch range without securing your foundation?
Go back to the basics. Build the base. Let growth come naturally.

5th POSSESSION

Proper Spacing

Basketball Theory

Floor spacing keeps one defender from guarding two offensive players. Proper spacing creates lanes for movement, vision, and opportunity. It allows the ball to move freely and players to operate with purpose. A crowded floor invites turnovers, rushed decisions, and stagnant offense. Even talented teams struggle when spacing collapses because options disappear. Spacing is not accidental. It is intentional positioning that gives everyone room to do their job well.

Life Application

Life works the same way. Organization creates freedom. When your life is overcrowded, clarity disappears. Reduce clutter. Write things down. Build systems. Separate responsibilities. Delegate tasks when appropriate. Structure creates lanes to move forward. Without it, even capable people feel overwhelmed, distracted, and stuck. Space is not wasted capacity. It is necessary capacity.

Hardwood Insight

Great teams do not magically have more space than everyone else. They create it intentionally. They understand where to stand, when to move, and how to clear areas so teammates can operate. Spacing is a discipline, not a luxury.

Real-Life Parallel

Many people are stuck not because they lack ability, but because their lives are too cluttered to execute. Too many commitments. Too many distractions. Too many unfinished tasks competing for attention. Progress stalls when everything is crowded and nothing has room to breathe.

Leadership Insight

Strong leaders create structure so people can thrive. They define roles, clarify priorities, and remove unnecessary confusion. Confusion drains energy and creates frustration. Clarity multiplies effort and momentum. Leaders who organize well give others space to perform at their best.

The Squeak

Make room to move. Progress requires space. When everything is crowded, movement becomes forced and inefficient. Creating space is an act of discipline and intention. Whether on the floor or in life, room to move allows vision, timing, and opportunity to line up. Clear space creates flow. Clear your mind and make room for creativity, strategic thinking, and innovation.

The Next Play

What area of your life needs better organization so progress can flow again?
What clutter needs to be cleared so you can see the lane more clearly?
Create space. Make room to move. Let momentum return.

6th POSSESSION

Counter Moves

Basketball Theory

Smart players always have a counter. If the defender takes away your first move, you cannot freeze or force it. You need another option. You must have a bag with more than one answer. One move may get you started, but counters keep you effective. Defenses adjust quickly, and players who rely on a single trick become predictable. Having a counter means you are prepared, composed, and able to respond instead of react. It is the difference between being skilled and being dangerous.

Life Application

Life requires the same flexibility. Multiple skills. Multiple paths forward. When one door closes, progress does not have to stop. You keep moving because you are not dependent on one outcome. Growth belongs to those who recognize the obstacle, respond with intention, and revise their approach without losing momentum. Adaptability is not quitting. It is wisdom in motion.

Hardwood Insight

One-move players are easy to stop. Once the defense knows what is coming, the advantage disappears. Players with counters force defenders to hesitate, adjust, and stay honest. Depth creates opportunity.

Real-Life Parallel

If your entire future depends on one plan, pressure will crush you.
When that plan hits resistance, panic sets in. Depth creates
resilience. Make your main thing the main thing, but it is wise to
develop additional skills, options, and perspectives. Counters keep
you moving when conditions change.

Leadership Insight

Strong leaders prepare contingencies. They respect reality enough to
plan for it. They understand that circumstances shift, people change,
and plans encounter resistance. Leaders with counters do not panic
when Plan A stalls. They adjust, reframe, and continue forward with
clarity and confidence.

The Squeak

Have a counter ready. Do not let resistance stop your momentum.
Preparation gives you options, and options keep you in control.
When your first move is taken away, your response reveals your
readiness. Depth turns obstacles into opportunities to advance.

The Next Play

If your first plan fails, what is next?
What option have you prepared so you are not forced into
desperation or delay?
Develop your counter now so you are ready when resistance shows
up.

7th POSSESSION

Stay Ready

Basketball Theory

Prepared players stay engaged. They warm up with purpose, pay attention to the flow of the game, and stay mentally connected even when they are not on the floor. When their number is called, there is no panic and no scramble. They are ready because they never checked out. Readiness is not accidental. It is the result of intentional preparation before the moment arrives.

Life Application

Life works the same way. If you stay ready, you will not have to get ready. Keeping your life in order positions you to respond calmly instead of reacting desperately. When opportunity shows up, you do not rush to catch up. You step forward with confidence because you are already in position. Opportunities are often brief and unforgiving. They favor the prepared and pass over the distracted. Readiness turns opportunity into momentum.

Hardwood Insight

Readiness creates quiet confidence. Players who are prepared do not need to announce themselves. They move with composure because they trust their preparation. Confidence grows when you know you have done the work long before your name is called.

Real-Life Parallel

Opportunities come fast and rarely on schedule. If you are always getting ready, you will always be late. Many missed opportunities are not about lack of talent, but lack of readiness. Staying prepared allows you to act while others are still organizing.

Leadership Insight

Strong leaders live prepared. They build systems, anticipate challenges, and think ahead before opportunities or emergencies arrive. Preparation allows leaders to respond with clarity instead of chaos. When pressure hits, prepared leaders steady the room because they have already considered the moment.

The Squeak

Stay ready. Do not make the coach, or life, call your name twice. Readiness is respect for the moment before it arrives. It signals discipline, attentiveness, and seriousness. When you stay ready, you honor opportunity and position yourself to contribute immediately.

The Next Play

What area of your life needs tightening right now so you are ready when the call comes?
What would change if you prepared today for an opportunity that has not arrived yet?
Stay ready. Be positioned. When your name is called, step in with confidence.

8th POSSESSION

Don't Let the Clock Rush You

Basketball Theory

Do not let the clock cause you to abandon your routine. Great players still breathe, square up, and trust their mechanics even when time is short. Panic rushes. Routine steadies.

Life Application

Take your time. Be methodical. Work your process. Pressure does not require panic; it requires focus. When the moment feels rushed, slow your thinking and trust what you've practiced. Stay disciplined, let preparation guide your execution, and allow clarity to carry you through high-pressure moments. Remember, until the clock hits zero, there's still time to make the right play.

Hardwood Insight

When players rush, everything gets sloppy. Footwork breaks down. Shot selection deteriorates. Passes sail. When players trust their routine, the game slows down. Movements stay sharp. Decisions stay clean. Rushing is usually a sign of insecurity or panic. Trusting mechanics is a sign of preparation. Players who rely on their fundamentals allow the game to come to them instead of trying to outrun it.

Real-Life Parallel

Life will put you on a clock. Deadlines, expectations, and pressure are unavoidable. When urgency rises, the temptation is to abandon your process and react emotionally. That shortcut almost always creates chaos. Rushing trades clarity for speed and control for impulse. People who trust their process stay grounded when pressure hits. They execute what they know instead of scrambling for what they feel.

Leadership Insight

Strong leaders slow moments down and make the next best decision, not the fastest one. They understand that urgency does not equal wisdom. They resist the pressure to react and instead respond with composure, clarity, decisiveness, and deliberate steps, especially when they are feeling rushed. Leadership is revealed in how calmly and clearly you move when everyone else feels pressed.

The Squeak

Trust your mechanics. Pressure exposes whether you prepared or panicked. Mechanics are what you fall back on when emotions are high and time feels short. When you trust what you have trained, you regain control of the moment. Rushing feels productive, but execution wins possessions. Trusting your mechanics keeps you steady when the clock is loud.

The Next Play

Where are you rushing right now instead of executing your process? What would change if you slowed the moment down and trusted what you have already built?
Pause. Set your feet. Execute the next best step.

9th POSSESSION

Rest Properly

Basketball Theory

Rest is part of preparation. Smart players understand that recovery is not weakness, it is wisdom. Practices are intense. Games are demanding. Without proper rest, the body breaks down, decision-making slows, and performance declines. Coaches build rest into the schedule because availability tomorrow depends on recovery today.

Life Application

Shut it down willingly before your body does it for you. Rest is not quitting. Rest is stewardship. When you ignore exhaustion, you borrow energy you don't have and pay interest later. Intentional rest allows you to return focused, healthy, and effective instead of burned out and broken down.

Hardwood Insight

The players who last the longest are not the ones who grind nonstop. They are the ones who understand rhythm. They know when to push and when to recover. They practice hard, compete hard, and then shut it down with intention. Constant grinding dulls focus, weakens the body, and shortens careers. Longevity belongs to players who respect recovery as much as effort.

Real-Life Parallel

Many people wear exhaustion like a badge of honor until their health, relationships, or judgment collapse. Burnout is rarely sudden. It is the result of warning signs ignored over time. Fatigue clouds decision-making. Weariness erodes patience. Eventually, what started as dedication becomes damage. Rest is not quitting. It is maintenance.

Leadership Insight

Strong leaders model healthy rhythms. They give themselves permission to rest and give others permission to do the same. They understand that depleted people make poor decisions and fragile teams. Sustainable leadership requires recovery, margin, and space to reset. Leaders who never rest eventually force others to carry the cost.

The Squeak

Rest is part of the work. Recovery is not a reward for finishing. It is a requirement for continuing. Rest sharpens focus, restores strength, and protects judgment. Players who respect rest extend their effectiveness. Leaders who honor recovery preserve their capacity to lead well over time.

The Next Play

Where do you need to shut it down before damage sets in?
What boundary needs to be established so rest becomes intentional instead of forced?
Schedule recovery on purpose so your body, mind, or relationships do not demand it later.

10ᵗʰ POSSESSION

Study the Film

Basketball Theory

Great players study film. They watch possessions over and over, not to admire highlights but to identify mistakes, tendencies, and missed opportunities. Film doesn't lie. It shows footwork, spacing, effort, body language, and decision-making exactly as they happened. Studying film turns experience into instruction.

Life Application

Life requires self-reflection, accountability, and introspection. If you never slow down to examine your choices, patterns, and reactions, you'll keep repeating the same mistakes. Growth demands honesty. Reviewing your life with clarity allows you to adjust, mature, and improve intentionally.

Hardwood Insight

Players who refuse to watch film rarely change. They keep repeating the same mistakes because they never face what is actually happening. But players who embrace film improve faster because they are willing to confront reality. Film does not care about excuses. It shows effort, positioning, decision-making, and habits. It reveals what you did, not what you meant to do. And once you see it clearly, you can correct it. Film turns vague feelings into specific adjustments.

Real-Life Parallel

Many people move from moment to moment without ever evaluating what went wrong or what went right. They stay busy, stay distracted, and then wonder why nothing changes. Reflection turns experience into wisdom. Avoidance keeps you stuck. Without review, life becomes repetition. When you take time to look honestly at your choices, you stop living on autopilot and start living with intention.

Leadership Insight

Strong leaders regularly assess themselves. They own mistakes, correct blind spots, and adjust direction before problems compound. They do not wait for failure to force reflection. They build reflection into the routine. Accountability always starts at the top because leaders set the tone. A leader who refuses self-review creates a culture where nobody grows. A leader who reviews honestly creates a culture of improvement.

The Squeak

Review before you repeat. If you do not examine your habits, you will keep rehearsing them. Film study is not punishment. It is preparation. It is the discipline of looking at yourself clearly enough to grow. The goal is not shame. The goal is change. Reviewing the truth gives you power to adjust the future.

The Next Play

What decision, habit, or pattern needs honest review right now? What are you repeating because you have not stopped to evaluate it? Take time to look at it clearly, own it fully, and adjust accordingly.

GAME CHANGING PLAY

Handling Crowd Noise

Every game has noise. Some of it is supportive. Some of it is hostile. But none of it is accidental.

On the road, the crowd has one primary agenda: to get you off your game. They want to rush you, distract you, frustrate you, and pull you out of rhythm. They boo calls. They celebrate mistakes. They apply pressure not with talent, but with volume. Great teams understand this. They don't react emotionally. They don't argue with officials. They don't play faster than they should. They quiet the crowd the only way that works, by executing, staying disciplined, and playing their game possession by possession.

At home, the crowd serves a different purpose. A home crowd can become an extra player on the floor. Their energy fuels momentum. Their presence lifts you when your legs are heavy and your shots aren't falling. A well-timed roar can spark a run. A standing ovation can restore confidence. Smart teams know how to draw strength from their crowd without becoming dependent on it.

The key is discernment.

Not all noise deserves the same response. Some noise must be ignored. Other noise should be embraced. Championship-level players know the difference.

Life works the same way.

Life is full of voices, opinions, criticism, and advice. Some of it exists for the same reason as a hostile road crowd: to get you off your game. Critics, doubters, and enemies are often loud, persistent, and relentless. If you allow those voices to dictate your rhythm, you'll rush decisions, abandon your process, and lose clarity. Wisdom knows when to block the noise out completely.

But not all voices are enemies.

There are voices in your life meant to strengthen you. Mentors.
Coaches. Trusted friends. People who have already won in areas
where you're still learning. Ignoring those voices is just as dangerous
as listening to the wrong ones. Growth requires humility. Progress
requires teachability. And success often requires listening to
someone who sees the game more clearly than you do.

The mistake many people make is treating all noise the same. They
either listen to everything or shut everything out. Both approaches
lead to confusion. Discernment is learning which voices sharpen you
and which ones are trying to rattle you.

When you master crowd noise, you stay composed on the road and
energized at home. You don't play to the noise. You don't perform for
approval. You stay grounded in your preparation, your values, and
your purpose.

And when you do that, noise either loses its power or serves its
purpose.

That's a game changer.

SPECIAL
PRESENTATION

ODE TO THE BALL

You were there from the very beginning.

I bounced you before I understood rhythm. I shot you before I understood form. I spun you on my finger just to see if I could. I put you between my legs and behind my back, not because it was necessary, but because it felt good.

I passed you to others and trusted you would come back to me. Sometimes you did. Sometimes you didn't. And I learned from both.

I sat on couches and floors watching games with you resting beside me, like a loyal companion who never needed to speak. I carried you into driveways, playgrounds, and gyms. I introduced you to my kids. I let them hold you, bounce you, and feel what I felt, hoping you would teach them something too.

I used you to impress fans and catch attention. I dunked you when my legs were young. I tossed you into the air in victorious celebration. I kicked you in frustration when things didn't go my way.

You never complained.

I leaned on you during heartbreak and loss. I used you as my voice when words failed me. I used you to move the crowd, to create energy, to feel alive when life felt heavy.

I owe you apologies.

For every layup I missed. For every free throw I left short. Even for the occasional airballs. For every careless turnover. For the days I took you for granted and assumed you'd always be there.

You didn't owe me anything. But you gave me everything you had.

You paid for my education. You made my family proud of me. You introduced me to some amazing people, places, and things. You stayed faithful even when my role changed.

You were always the star. And without you, there was no game. No me.

Thank you for being patient. Thank you for being reliable. Thank you for always bouncing back, even when I didn't.

Thank you for riding with me.

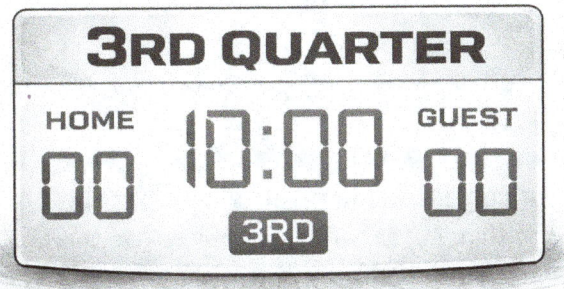

Effort, Energy, & Pace

1st POSSESSION

Have A Motor

Basketball Theory

A motor is your consistent energy level. It is not emotion and it is not hype. Players with a motor bring effort every possession, every drill, every game. They run the floor, contest shots, chase rebounds, and stay engaged even when the ball is not in their hands. A strong motor does not depend on mood or circumstances. It depends on commitment. Motors show up when legs are tired, shots are not falling, and recognition is minimal. Coaches trust motors because motors are reliable.

Life Application

Life rewards the same consistency. Approach life with enthusiasm, not because every day is exciting, but because energy creates momentum. Effort opens doors that talent alone cannot. When you consistently bring energy to your work, your relationships, and your responsibilities, people notice. Opportunities often come not to the most gifted, but to the most engaged. Energy signals readiness.

Hardwood Insight

Coaches cannot teach motor. They can only reward it. Skill can be developed and schemes can be learned, but effort is a choice. Players with a motor always find minutes because they affect the game even when they are not scoring. Energy changes possessions.

Real-Life Parallel

Many people have ability but lack energy. They show up tired, disengaged, and half-present. Over time, that costs them influence, trust, and opportunity. People are drawn to energy because energy creates movement. A lack of energy quietly limits growth, even when talent is present.

Leadership Insight

Leaders set the emotional temperature. When leaders bring consistent energy, teams respond with focus and engagement. When leaders are flat, distracted, or passive, organizations drift. Energy does not mean constant intensity. It means intentional presence. Leaders who bring energy give people permission to care.

The Squeak

Bring it every possession. Motors separate contributors from observers. Energy is not something you wait to feel. It is something you decide to bring. When effort is consistent, confidence grows and opportunity expands. A strong motor makes you useful in every situation, even when conditions are not ideal.

The Next Play

Where do you need to raise your energy level instead of waiting to feel motivated?
What would change if you chose engagement over convenience today?
Bring it. Every possession counts.

2nd POSSESSION

Play With Pace and Tempo

Basketball Theory

Great teams understand pace and tempo. Sometimes you push the ball and attack early, before the defense gets set. Other times you slow the game down, value the possession, and execute with precision. Wisdom is knowing the difference. Playing fast without control leads to turnovers and rushed shots. Playing slow without intention leads to stagnation and wasted possessions. Tempo is not about speed alone. It is about command. Teams that control tempo control the game.

Life Application

Life works the same way. Not every season requires the same speed. Some moments demand urgency, boldness, and decisive action. Others require patience, reflection, and restraint. Problems arise when you treat every situation the same. Wisdom is recognizing the moment you are in and responding appropriately. Knowing when to accelerate and when to slow down protects both progress and peace.

Hardwood Insight

The best point guards do not just move fast. They move smart. They read the floor, sense momentum, and dictate pace instead of reacting to it. They understand when to attack and when to pull it back. Control, not speed, is what makes them effective.

Real-Life Parallel

Burnout often comes from running at one speed all the time. Constant urgency exhausts judgment. Constant caution kills momentum. Sustainable success requires variation in tempo. Those who last learn how to press without panicking and rest without disengaging.

Leadership Insight

Strong leaders control pace. They know when to press an issue and when to pause for clarity. They do not confuse urgency with recklessness or patience with passivity. Leaders who manage tempo well create environments that are both productive and healthy. They move organizations forward without running people into the ground.

The Squeak

Control the tempo. Do not let circumstances rush you or fear slow you down. Tempo is a leadership skill. When you control pace, you protect decision-making, preserve energy, and maximize effectiveness. The leader who controls tempo keeps the team balanced and the mission on track.

The Next Play

Where do you need to speed up right now and act with boldness? Where do you need to slow down and execute with greater intention?
Adjust the pace. Control the tempo. Play the moment you are in.

3rd POSSESSION

Run The Floor

Basketball Theory

No one can go all out all the time. There are moments in basketball when jogging is permissible, such as getting organized between plays or flowing into the offense. But jogging is never acceptable on a fast break. When the ball is pushed up the floor, the wings have to run. The lane runner has to sprint. Fast breaks reward urgency. Players who run the floor hard often get the easiest shots in the game: uncontested layups.

Jogging on a fast break doesn't conserve energy. It wastes opportunity.

Life Application

Don't go through life at half speed just going through the motions. There are seasons to rest, recover, and catch your breath. But when opportunity breaks loose, you have to move with urgency. Go hard when it's time to go hard. Rest fully when it's time to rest. Half-effort during opportunity produces half-results.

Hardwood Insight

Coaches forgive missed shots. They do not forgive jogging on a fast break. A missed shot can happen to anyone. Jogging back on a fast break is a choice. Sprinting signals hunger, awareness, and readiness. It shows you recognize the moment and respect the opportunity. Fast breaks are fleeting. They reward players who react instantly and punish those who hesitate. Effort and urgency turn advantage into points.

Real-Life Parallel

Many people miss open doors not because they lack ability, but because they move too slowly when opportunity appears. Timing matters. Opportunities rarely wait for you to feel ready. They show up suddenly and demand immediate response. Hesitation turns opportunity into regret. Those who recognize the break and sprint capitalize before the window closes.

Leadership Insight

Strong leaders recognize moments that require urgency. They know when deliberation is appropriate and when action is required. When the situation calls for speed, they shift gears decisively. Leaders who hesitate in fast-break moments allow momentum to die and opportunity to slip away. Urgency, when applied wisely, creates progress.

The Squeak

It is called a fast break for a reason. Some moments are not designed for caution or overthinking. They are designed for action. Sprinting does not mean recklessness. It means awareness and decisiveness. When opportunity is clearly in front of you, speed honors the moment. Jogging wastes it.

The Next Play

Where has opportunity opened up in your life that requires urgency instead of caution?
What would change if you stopped hesitating and started moving decisively?
When the break is on, sprint.

4th POSSESSION

Dive on Loose Balls

Basketball Theory

Loose balls are 50–50 opportunities. No play is drawn for them, and no guarantee exists that they will fall into your hands. Diving on the floor is a conscious decision to value possession over comfort. It is effort without applause and commitment without certainty. Teams that consistently win loose balls often win games because they understand a simple truth. Every possession matters, especially the ones no one expects you to get.

Life Application

Life presents the same kind of moments. Opportunities often appear small, inconvenient, or beneath notice. They rarely announce themselves as important. Letting them pass because they feel uncomfortable or insignificant creates regret later. Effort in overlooked moments builds momentum that cannot be manufactured later. Urgency separates those who advance from those who observe.

Hardwood Insight

Diving on the floor changes momentum. It energizes teammates and disrupts opponents. It sends a message that effort is non-negotiable and that nothing is being taken for granted. One loose ball can shift the tone of an entire game because it reveals who wants the moment more.

Real-Life Parallel

Small opportunities often lead to bigger ones. People who hesitate miss doors they never realize were opening. Advancement frequently begins with moments that feel minor but require decisive action. Those who move early position themselves for outcomes others never reach.

Leadership Insight

Strong leaders act decisively. They move when others hesitate and step into moments that are uncomfortable, uncertain, or unglamorous. Momentum is often created through effort, not authority. Leaders who value every possession set a standard that effort matters at every level.

The Squeak

Every possession matters. Some wins are loud, but many are earned on the floor. Diving on loose balls is about mindset, not highlight plays. When you consistently value effort over comfort, you separate yourself from those who wait for ideal conditions. Possessions add up, and so do the moments you choose to go get.

The Next Play

What opportunity is on the floor right now that you have been slow to pursue because it feels inconvenient or uncomfortable?
What would change if you decided to go get it instead of waiting for something cleaner?
Hit the floor. Secure the possession. Momentum follows effort.
act on?

5th POSSESSION

Cut With Intention

Basketball Theory

Cuts through the lane must be purposeful. There is no room for drifting or hesitation in the paint. Every cut should be sharp, decisive, and intentional. Eyes up. Hands ready. You cut expecting the ball because you might receive it at any moment. Scoring cuts are not accidental. They are made with awareness, timing, and readiness to finish. Players who cut with purpose put constant pressure on the defense and turn movement into opportunity.

Life Application

Life requires the same intentionality. Move with purpose. Walk like you are going somewhere. Make deliberate strides instead of meandering through days and decisions. When you move with clarity and direction, you position yourself to receive opportunities you would otherwise miss. Purposeful movement signals readiness. Drifting signals uncertainty.

Hardwood Insight

Coaches notice cutters who move with intent. They trust them because they know those players are alert, engaged, and prepared to capitalize on the moment. Lazy cuts clog the offense and waste possessions. Intentional cuts create points because they are timed, committed, and finished strong.

Real-Life Parallel

Many people miss opportunities not because they lack ability, but because they drift through life without direction. They are present but not prepared. They show up without expectation. Movement without intention rarely produces progress. Purpose creates alignment between effort and opportunity.

Leadership Insight

Strong leaders move deliberately. Their actions communicate direction, confidence, and readiness long before words ever do. Intentional movement builds credibility because it shows awareness of timing and responsibility. Leaders who drift create confusion. Leaders who move with purpose create momentum.

The Squeak

Cut to score. Do not move just to stay busy. Move with expectation. Purposeful cuts put you in position to receive, finish, and contribute. When you move intentionally, you tell the game, and life, that you are ready for the opportunity that may come at any moment.

The Next Play

Where are you drifting instead of moving with purpose right now? What area of your life needs a sharper, more intentional move? Choose one lane. Commit to the cut. Be ready to finish when the opportunity comes.

6th POSSESSION

Get Back on D!

Basketball Theory

Getting back on defense requires two things: effort and assessment. You have to sprint back hard, but you're not just running aimlessly. You're hustling with purpose. As you retreat, you're identifying who has the ball and locating the player you're responsible for guarding. You're calling out matchups, communicating, and stopping the ball. Defense breaks down when players jog back without awareness. Good defense begins the moment possession changes.

Life Application

When circumstances change, respond with urgency and clarity. Life shifts quickly. A setback, a mistake, or an unexpected turn requires immediate effort, but also thoughtful assessment. You have to move fast while identifying priorities, responsibilities, and next steps. Panic reacts. Discipline responds.

Hardwood Insight

Coaches do not just yell "get back" for noise. They want communication. They want awareness. They want players sprinting with their heads up, not just their legs moving. Hustle without thinking still leads to breakdowns. Players who run hard but lose track of their assignment give up easy baskets. Recovery defense requires urgency *and* recognition. The goal is not frantic movement. The goal is effective response.

Real-Life Parallel

Life works the same way when things go wrong. Some people freeze and do nothing. Others overreact and create more damage. The best responses combine effort with awareness. They move quickly while thinking clearly. Speed without direction creates chaos. Awareness without action creates delay. Progress happens when urgency and clarity work together.

Leadership Insight

Strong leaders stabilize situations under pressure. They hustle to address the issue, but they do not abandon judgment. They assess what is happening, identify priorities, and assign responsibility. Leaders who stay calm while moving decisively prevent small problems from becoming full-scale breakdowns. Presence under pressure builds confidence in everyone watching.

The Squeak

Respond with awareness. Hustle matters, but awareness directs it. Sprinting without understanding wastes energy. Thinking without movement wastes time. The best responses balance urgency with clarity. When you move fast *and* think clearly, you protect the possession and stabilize the moment.

The Next Play

Where do you need to respond quickly while also thinking clearly right now?
What situation requires urgency without panic?
Hustle back. Assess the situation. Take responsibility for your assignment.

7th POSSESSION

Take the Charge

Basketball Theory

Taking a charge requires commitment. You have to move your feet, get in position, and plant yourself before the contact comes. Then you brace for impact and put your body on the line. Taking a charge isn't flashy, and it's rarely comfortable, but it stops momentum and shifts the game. It's a decision to sacrifice personal comfort for the good of the team.

Life Application

Grounded people live sacrificially. They don't avoid responsibility when it's inconvenient or uncomfortable. They step into difficult moments, absorb pressure, and protect others when needed. Living with integrity often requires taking hits so others don't have to.

Hardwood Insight

Teammates remember who takes charges. It is one of the quickest ways to earn trust and respect because everyone knows that player is willing to do the hard, unseen work. Taking a charge requires anticipation, courage, and sacrifice. There is no glamour in it. Often it hurts. But it changes momentum and protects the team. Players who take charges communicate something without saying a word. They are committed to the collective, not personal comfort.

Real-Life Parallel

Life presents moments that feel just as uncomfortable. In families, workplaces, and communities, progress often depends on someone willing to step in when things get messy. Avoidance shifts the burden to others. Sacrifice absorbs it. Taking responsibility may not feel fair, but it often prevents greater damage. Someone has to stop the momentum going the wrong way.

Leadership Insight

Strong leaders step into pressure instead of deflecting it. They do not hide when outcomes are uncertain or consequences are heavy. They take responsibility for results and shield their people when necessary. Leadership often requires absorbing impact so others can stay positioned and focused. That willingness builds loyalty and long-term trust.

The Squeak

Take the hit. Leadership is not about avoiding discomfort. It is about protecting what matters most. When you step in front of pressure, you change the direction of the moment. Sacrifice does not weaken leadership. It strengthens it. Teams remember who was willing to stand in the lane when it counted.

The Next Play

Where is a sacrificial decision required of you right now?
What responsibility are you tempted to avoid because it feels costly or uncomfortable?
Step in. Take the hit. Do what is right for the team.

8th POSSESSION

Extending a Hand

Basketball Theory

When a teammate hits the floor, you don't stand over them or wait for the play to stop. You sprint over and extend a hand. Helping a teammate up is instinctive in good teams. It restores dignity, reinforces unity, and communicates, "You're not alone." It doesn't matter whose fault it was or how they fell. What matters is that they get back up.

Life Application

Don't look down on fallen people. Show compassion. We're teammates in humanity. Comrades of the human race. Teammates in the game of life. Everyone stumbles. Everyone falls. Extending yourself to help someone up is not weakness. It's strength expressed through empathy.

Hardwood Insight

Teams with strong culture help each other up without hesitation. When a teammate hits the floor, someone is already reaching down before the whistle blows. That instinct matters. It builds trust, reinforces belonging, and keeps players engaged after mistakes, collisions, or hard moments. Helping someone up communicates, *You're still with us.* It prevents shame from turning into disengagement and keeps the team connected possession after possession.

Real-Life Parallel

Life works the same way. People remember who helped them when they were down. Compassion shown in someone's lowest moment often becomes the bridge that restores hope, confidence, and momentum. A timely word, a steady presence, or a simple act of support can keep someone from checking out completely. Encouragement does not erase the fall, but it helps people rise faster.

Leadership Insight

Strong leaders lead with empathy. They correct when necessary, but they also lift, restore, and encourage. They understand that accountability without compassion breeds fear, while compassion without accountability breeds complacency. Leadership that balances both creates growth. Leaders who only criticize eventually lose people. Leaders who help others get back up build loyalty and resilience.

The Squeak

Pick each other up. Culture is revealed in how a team responds to failure and pain. Reaching down does not excuse the mistake. It reinforces commitment. When you help someone up, you keep them connected to the mission and remind them they still matter. Teams that lift each other recover faster and stay stronger longer.

The Next Play

Who around you has fallen and needs a hand instead of a lecture right now?
What would change if you moved toward them instead of standing back?
Extend yourself. Help them up. Strong teams rise together.

9th POSSESSION

Help and Recover

Basketball Theory

Help and recover is team defense at its best. When a teammate gets beat off the dribble, you slide over to stop penetration while still keeping your own assignment in view. You help just long enough to slow the ball, then you recover back to your responsibility. It requires hustle, communication, trust, and shared philosophy. When all five players commit to help and recover, defense moves as one unit. It's not five defenders. It's one defense.

Life Application

Healthy lives and healthy communities work the same way. You step in when someone needs help, but you don't abandon your own responsibilities in the process. Support does not mean rescue. Assistance does not mean neglecting your role. Maturity is knowing when to help and when to recover.

Hardwood Insight

Great defensive teams do not panic when someone gets beat. They trust the system and they trust each other. Help comes immediately, not emotionally. A teammate slides over, cuts off the lane, and stops the ball. Just as important, recovery follows just as fast. The original defender sprints back to their assignment, and the defense resets. Help defense only works when recovery is disciplined. Without recovery, help turns into scrambling and breakdowns.

Real-Life Parallel

Life requires the same balance. In families, friendships, and workplaces, people will occasionally get beat. Someone will fall short, make a mistake, or need assistance. Helping matters, but so does knowing when to return to your role. Overextending yourself leads to burnout. Withholding help leads to isolation. Wisdom lives in the middle. Healthy relationships are built on support that does not abandon responsibility.

Leadership Insight

Strong leaders build cultures where people help without enabling and support without losing accountability. They clarify roles so help strengthens the system instead of weakening it. Everyone knows when to step in and when to rotate back. Leaders protect the whole by encouraging responsibility alongside compassion. When help and recovery are both practiced, teams stay strong, balanced, and connected.

The Squeak

Help, then recover. Support is powerful when it is paired with discipline. Helping does not mean abandoning your post. Recovery ensures that the system remains intact. Whether on defense or in life, balance comes from knowing when to step in and when to get back to your assignment. That awareness keeps everyone covered.

The Next Play

Who needs your help right now, and where do you need to recover back to your own responsibility?
Where might you be overhelping or under helping?
Step in wisely. Recover quickly. Stay disciplined in your role.

10th POSSESSION

Three-Man Weave

Basketball Theory

The three-man weave demands coordination, hustle, and care for the ball. Everyone sprints. Everyone exchanges the ball cleanly. Everyone makes the proper cut behind in sequence. If one player jogs, misses a pass, or cuts lazily, the drill breaks down. When done right, the three-man weave looks smooth, connected, and rhythmic because all three players are committed to the same pattern and purpose.

Life Application

Life works best when people move together with shared understanding. Progress requires cooperation, communication, and trust. You have to do your part, at the right time, in the right order, while respecting the roles of others. When people rush ahead, lag behind, or ignore the process, momentum is lost.

Hardwood Insight

Coaches use the three-man weave to teach more than passing. They use it to teach responsibility, timing, spacing, and awareness of others. Every player has a role. Every cut matters. If one person rushes, drifts, or freelances, the drill breaks down. The weave only works when players move in rhythm, trust the sequence, and honor their responsibility within it. It is a lesson in shared execution, not individual flair.

Real-Life Parallel

Life works the same way. Families, teams, and organizations break down when individuals refuse to move in sync. When people operate on their own timelines, priorities, or agendas, confusion replaces coordination. Success comes when individuals understand the sequence, respect timing, and honor the process. Moving together creates flow. Moving independently creates friction.

Leadership Insight

Strong leaders value alignment. They make sure everyone understands the plan, the pace, and their role within it. Alignment turns effort into progress. Without it, even hard work is wasted. Leaders who clarify direction and expectations allow people to move confidently instead of colliding with one another. Alignment does not limit people. It empowers them.

The Squeak

Move together. Progress is rarely a solo act. When people move in rhythm, momentum builds naturally. Coordination creates trust, and trust accelerates execution. Whether on the court or in life, shared movement produces better outcomes than isolated effort.

The Next Play

Where in your life is coordination breaking down right now?
What conversation, clarification, or adjustment is needed to restore rhythm?
Slow it down. Reestablish alignment. Commit to moving together.

GAME CHANGING PLAY

Move Without the Ball

Late in the game, everyone wants the ball. But not everyone knows what to do when they don't have it.

In basketball, moving without the ball is a mark of intelligence and maturity. It means you understand spacing, timing, and purpose. You don't stand and watch. You don't sulk because the play wasn't called for you. You cut hard. You set screens. You relocate. You stay active. You create opportunities, even when your name isn't being called. Great players know that movement without the ball often creates the play that wins the game.

Most baskets are the result of someone else's movement.

A well-timed cut pulls a defender out of position. A screen frees a shooter. A simple relocation opens a driving lane. None of those plays show up as the final shot, but without them, the shot never happens. Teams that win understand this. They trust that if they keep moving with purpose, the ball will find the right place at the right time.

Life works the same way.

There will be seasons when you are not in the spotlight. When you are not leading the meeting. When you are not making the final decision. When your contribution feels unseen. These moments reveal whether you are committed to the mission or attached to attention. People who only know how to function when they have control struggle in these seasons. People who know how to move without the ball continue to grow.

Moving without the ball in life means staying engaged even when you're not featured. It means supporting others without jealousy. It means adding value without needing credit. It means trusting that your preparation and posture still matter, even when the ball isn't in your hands. These are the people teams rely on. These are the people leaders trust. These are the people who stay ready for the moment when responsibility returns.

Standing still helps no one.

When you stop moving, you clog the lane. You shrink the floor. You limit possibilities. The same is true in life. When you disengage, withdraw, or wait to be noticed, opportunities stall. Growth slows. Momentum dies. Purpose requires motion, even in the background.

Moving without the ball also requires humility. It requires confidence that is not tied to applause. It requires understanding that winning is bigger than individual recognition. In the fourth quarter of life, that wisdom matters more than raw talent.

Here's the truth.
The ball always finds movers.

Not immediately. Not on demand. But eventually. People who stay active, intentional, and unselfish are always positioned for opportunity. When the defense shifts. When the moment opens. When the game calls for someone ready.

The final moments don't belong to the loudest player.
They belong to the most prepared one.

If you can move without the ball, you can be trusted with it.

That's a game changer

Awareness & Wisdom

1st POSSESSION

Stop the Ball

Basketball Theory

On defense, the first priority is stopping the ball. The player with the ball is the most immediate threat to score, and everything else flows from that reality. Good defenders do not drift, reach, or guess. They close space with urgency, get low, stay balanced, and force the ball handler to change direction. Help defense matters, rotations matter, and schemes matter, but none of it works if the ball is allowed to penetrate freely. You stop the ball first, then you worry about everything else.

Life Application

When a crisis hits, clarity begins with addressing what is most immediate. Too often, people try to solve secondary problems while the primary issue continues to cause damage. You cannot strategize effectively while the situation is still bleeding. Progress starts by handling what is right in front of you. Deal with the urgent issue first, then move forward with intention.

Hardwood Insight

Great teams do not panic under pressure. They stop the ball first, then get organized. By neutralizing the biggest threat, they force the offense to slow down, communicate more, and work deeper into the possession. This allows defenders to get into proper position, talk through assignments, and regain control without guessing or scrambling. Stopping the ball creates order.

Real-Life Parallel

Many people become overwhelmed because they try to fix everything at once. That approach creates confusion, fatigue, and poor decisions. Momentum is built by identifying the most urgent matter, addressing it decisively, and then moving to the next priority from a position of control instead of chaos.

Leadership Insight

Strong leaders triage effectively. They assess situations quickly, identify the greatest threat, and take immediate action to stabilize conditions. They do not ignore long-term vision, but they understand that stability must come before expansion. Leadership begins with control.

The Squeak

Somebody has to step up and stop the ball. It cannot be everybody, and it cannot be nobody. On every possession, one defender must take responsibility, absorb the pressure, and say, "I've got it." Will it be you?

The Next Play

What immediate issue is demanding your attention right now that you have been avoiding or hoping someone else would handle?
If nothing changes, what damage will continue to spread?
What would happen if you stepped up, addressed the problem directly, and forced momentum to shift?

2nd POSSESSION

A Bad Shot Is Better Than a Turnover

Basketball Theory

A bad shot still gives your team a chance. A turnover gives the opponent the ball outright. Smart players understand the value of possession. While shot selection matters, hesitation, carelessness, and poor awareness often lead to turnovers that cost games. Coaches would rather live with a bad shot than a careless pass, travel, or violation caused by uncertainty. Possession is currency. Once you give it away, you surrender control. Take the shot because sometimes, even bad shots go in.

Life Application

Taking imperfect action is often better than doing nothing. Fear of making mistakes can stall progress and trap people in overthinking. Growth happens through movement, adjustment, and learning along the way. While wisdom calls for restraint at times, constant hesitation creates missed opportunities. Learn as you move forward, but avoid decisions that create unnecessary damage or long-term consequences.

Hardwood Insight

Coaches can live with a bad shot. They can correct mechanics, timing, and shot selection. What frustrates teams is giving the ball away through carelessness, hesitation, or poor awareness. Turnovers hand possession to the opponent without a fight and often shift momentum. Possessions are precious, and smart teams protect them.

Real-Life Parallel

Waiting for perfect clarity often leads to missed opportunities. Life rarely provides full certainty before action is required. Responsible action beats paralysis. Momentum is built by stepping forward, learning, and refining course along the way.

Leadership Insight

Strong leaders act decisively while remaining teachable. They weigh risks, make informed choices, and move forward without needing perfect conditions. They avoid reckless decisions, but they also refuse to freeze under pressure. Leadership requires judgment, courage, and ownership of outcomes.

The Squeak

Protect possession.

The Next Play

What are you quietly giving away right now through hesitation, carelessness, or inaction?
When this opportunity is gone, what will you regret more, the shot you took and missed or the possession and opportunity you squandered by never taking it?

3rd POSSESSION

Situational Awareness

Basketball Theory

Great players are never guessing. They know the score, the time on the clock, the foul situation, and who is on the floor with them. They understand whether the moment calls for patience or urgency, control or aggression. Awareness determines decision-making. A good play made in the wrong moment quickly becomes a bad one. Situational awareness is what keeps a player from forcing shots, committing unnecessary fouls, or making risky passes when the game does not require it.

Life Application

Life demands the same level of awareness. Your relationships, finances, health, and responsibilities are all connected to timing and context. What is wise in one season can be reckless in another. Pay attention to what is happening around you and within you. Context matters. Decisions made without awareness often create avoidable stress, damaged trust, and unnecessary consequences.

Hardwood Insight

Basketball IQ separates good players from great ones. Talent can get you on the court, but awareness keeps you there. Players who understand the game make fewer mistakes, elevate their teammates, and consistently put themselves in the right position at the right time.

Real-Life Parallel

Many mistakes in life do not come from bad intentions. They come from poor awareness. Missed signals, ignored warning signs, and rushed decisions often lead to outcomes that could have been avoided if someone had simply slowed down and paid attention.

Leadership Insight

Effective leaders do not react blindly. They make informed decisions because they understand context, timing, and consequence. They read the room, recognize the moment, and adjust their approach accordingly. Leadership without awareness leads to missteps. Leadership with awareness builds trust and stability.

The Squeak

Know the situation. Talent without awareness is dangerous. Effort without context is inefficient. The best players are not just skilled, they are informed. They understand the score, the time, the fouls, the personnel, and the moment. They know when to push and when to pull back, when to attack and when to protect possession. Situational awareness keeps good intentions from becoming bad decisions. When you know the situation, you stop reacting and start responding with purpose.

The Next Play

What context are you overlooking right now that should be shaping your decisions?
What information are you ignoring because it complicates the choice you want to make?
What changes when you slow down, assess the moment honestly, and adjust your approach instead of forcing your preference?

4th POSSESSION

Touch Every Line

Basketball Theory

Gassers, 17's, and line runs require players to touch every line. No exceptions. Cutting corners does not count because conditioning is not about speed alone. It is about preparation. These drills are designed to train both body and mind for sudden changes, quick transitions, and moments when fatigue meets pressure. Full commitment matters because the game will eventually demand movements you cannot rehearse halfway. Conditioning exposes habits. Players who respect every line prepare themselves for the chaos of real competition.

Life Application

Life requires the same level of engagement. Growth comes from embracing the full range of experiences, not selectively choosing only the enjoyable ones. Blessings, challenges, beauty, disappointment, success, and hardship all shape character. Skipping difficult seasons may feel easier in the moment, but it weakens development. The process works when it is honored in its entirety. Growth demands participation, not avoidance.

Hardwood Insight

"Everybody on the line!" Players who cut corners in conditioning may look fine early, but they struggle late in games. Fatigue exposes preparation. When legs get heavy and focus slips, those who avoided the work are revealed. Conditioning does not lie.

Real-Life Parallel

Avoidance delays maturity. Endurance is built through full engagement, not partial effort. Touch every moment life presents you. Some moments will stretch you. Some will exhaust you. Others may hurt deeply. But each one builds capacity, resilience, and staying power. Pain is not always punishment. Often, it is preparation.

Leadership Insight

Leaders do not grow around adversity. They grow through it. Pressure develops discernment. Resistance builds strength. Difficulty clarifies values. Leaders who face challenges head-on emerge steadier, wiser, and more capable of guiding others through similar terrain.

The Squeak

Finish the conditioning. Anyone can start the drill. Anyone can look strong in the first few reps. Conditioning reveals itself later, when fatigue sets in and effort becomes a choice. Finishing the conditioning is about respect for the process and honesty with yourself. It is a refusal to cut corners when no one is watching. Those who finish the work build endurance, discipline, and confidence that shows up when it matters most.

The Next Play

What part of the process are you tempted to skip right now because it is uncomfortable, inconvenient, or demanding more than you want to give?
What growth, strength, or maturity is waiting on the other side of that unfinished work?
Step into it. Stay with it. Do the work all the way through.

5th POSSESSION

Protect the House

Basketball Theory

Home court matters. Teams play differently in their own gym. They know the rims. They know the floor. They feed off the crowd. Because of that, good teams take pride in defending their house. They don't allow opponents to come in comfortably, dictate tempo, or take what isn't theirs. Protecting the house is about pride, preparation, and presence. You defend your space because it represents who you are.

Life Application

Protect your home. Protect your family. Protect your peace. Guard what has been entrusted to you with intention and wisdom. That means prayer, love, boundaries, and yes, practical measures when necessary. Stewardship requires vigilance. What you don't protect, you eventually risk losing.

Hardwood Insight

Teams that consistently defend their home court build confidence, rhythm, and identity. They expect to win in their own gym because they have established standards there. When opponents are allowed to walk in comfortably and take control, belief starts to erode. Over time, losing at home weakens culture, disrupts momentum, and removes the psychological edge that home court is meant to provide.

Real-Life Parallel

Neglect creates vulnerability. When important areas of life are left unguarded, outside forces inevitably step in to influence direction and outcome. What begins as inattention often turns into erosion. Drift rarely announces itself, but it quietly **reshapes priorities,** compromises values, and creates problems that could have been prevented through consistent care.

Leadership Insight

Strong leaders do not only build systems, teams, and vision. They protect what they have built. They establish boundaries, reinforce standards, and address threats early before damage occurs. Leadership includes the responsibility to guard people, values, and environments so that growth can be sustained and trust remains intact.

The Squeak

Defend your space. What you allow access to will eventually influence you. Strong teams protect their home court because it represents identity, pride, and standard. In the same way, your space reflects what you value. Defending it is not about fear or control. It is about stewardship. When you fail to guard what matters, you silently invite disruption. Protection is an active responsibility, not a passive hope.

The Next Play

What area of your life needs better protection right now because it has been left exposed or taken for granted?
What boundaries need to be reinforced before pressure arrives?
Secure it now, while you have the advantage, not after it has already been tested.

6th POSSESSION

Finish the Play

Basketball Theory

Defense does not end when the shot goes up. It ends when the shot is made or missed and the rebound is secured. Too many possessions are lost because players relax too soon. They contest the shot, then stop. Winning teams finish the play. They track the ball, put a body on someone, and fight for position until possession is decided. Effort without completion leaves the door open for second chances.

Life Application

Do not give up on things that matter until the matter is settled. Starting strong does not guarantee finishing well. Follow-through is what turns effort into results. Many failures do not happen at the beginning. They happen just before completion, when attention fades and discipline slips.

Hardwood Insight

Second-chance points usually come from unfinished effort. The rebound often goes to the player who stayed engaged one second longer than everyone else.

Real-Life Parallel

Projects, relationships, goals, and commitments all demand completion. Half-finished work creates loose ends, lingering problems, and unnecessary stress. What you leave incomplete often costs more than what you finish.

Leadership Insight

Strong leaders finish what they start. They see things through even when energy dips, obstacles appear, or momentum slows. Finishing builds credibility. It signals reliability and earns trust.

The Squeak

Secure the rebound. A defensive stop means nothing if the possession is not finished. Too many good efforts are wasted because someone relaxes too soon and leaves the job incomplete. Rebounding requires awareness, positioning, and a willingness to pursue the ball when others assume the play is over. Securing the rebound is about finishing strong. It is the difference between effort and results, between progress and relapse. Possession is not earned until the ball is controlled.

The Next Play

What have you started that still needs to be finished properly, not casually or eventually?
Where have you assumed the job was done when it still requires attention, discipline, or follow-through?
Close the loop. Secure the outcome. Complete the work while the ball is still in reach.

7th POSSESSION

Who Got Next?

Basketball Theory

"Who got next?" is a pickup basketball question loaded with meaning. On the surface, it is about order. It asks who owns the next game. But beneath that, it is really a question of readiness and opportunity. Once someone answers, the follow-up almost always comes: "You got 'em all?" In other words, do you already have your four teammates lined up, or are you still missing pieces?

That second question matters because it reveals intent. Players ask it because they are watching for an opening. They are listening for opportunity. They are looking to see if there is a gap they can fill. In pickup basketball, opportunity does not announce itself. You have to be paying attention, positioned, and ready to respond when the moment presents itself.

Sometimes, the person with next doesn't answer right away. They stay noncommittal. Not because they're dishonest, but because they're discerning. They're watching who walks into the gym. They're quietly evaluating who fits, who brings value, and who helps the team win. Until it's time to step on the floor, selections are often held close.

That's not selfish. That's stewardship of responsibility.

Life Application

Life has moments when discernment matters. You don't always owe immediate answers. Not every decision needs public disclosure before it's time. Wisdom sometimes requires observation, patience, and quiet evaluation before commitment.

Hardwood Insight

In pickup basketball, no one expects full disclosure early. That's understood. But discernment is not indecision. It has a purpose and a timeline.

Real-Life Parallel

In leadership, relationships, and opportunity, there are seasons when you're still gathering information. You're watching patterns, assessing character, and weighing alignment. That's not avoidance. That's preparation.

Leadership Insight

Strong leaders know when to observe quietly and when to speak clearly. They don't rush decisions that affect others, but they don't hide forever either.

The Squeak

Discernment has a season. Wisdom is not just knowing what to do, but knowing *when* to do it. Timing matters. What is right too early can be reckless. What is right too late can be wasted. Discernment recognizes that every decision lives inside a moment, and missing the moment can undermine the decision itself. Mature judgment pays attention to readiness, conditions, and consequence. Not every door should be forced, and not every delay is wisdom. Knowing the season keeps good intentions from becoming bad outcomes.

The Next Play

Where do you need more patience and discernment before committing? Take time to observe but be prepared to act when the moment arrives.

8th POSSESSION

Call the Lineup

Basketball Theory

Eventually, the person with next has to call the lineup. When it is time to step on the floor, names get spoken, positions get set, and everyone knows who is playing. At that point, clarity is not optional. It is required. You do not walk halfway onto the court still deciding. You do not leave people guessing while the ball is being checked. You call the lineup.

Why? Because confusion kills trust. A team cannot function when roles are unclear. Momentum stalls when players do not know whether they are in or out. Calling the lineup signals readiness, leadership, and accountability. It tells everyone involved that preparation is over and execution has begun.

Life Application

There comes a time when transparency is no longer a choice. When responsibility begins, clarity must follow. People deserve to know where they stand. Ambiguity might feel safer for the person holding the decision, but it creates anxiety and instability for everyone else. Clear communication provides direction, alignment, and confidence when it matters most.

Hardwood Insight

Discretion has a season. So does disclosure. Wise players know when to stay quiet and when to speak up. But once the game is ready to start, silence becomes disruptive. At that point, clarity is part of the responsibility.

Real-Life Parallel

Life works the same way. There are seasons for thinking, praying, evaluating, and watching. Those seasons matter. But once your decision affects other people, clarity becomes an obligation.

If you are leading a team, people need direction.
If you are in a relationship, people need honesty.
If you are making commitments, people need to know where they stand.

Withholding clarity past its proper moment is not wisdom. It is avoidance.

Leadership Insight

Strong leaders know the difference between protecting options and stringing people along. Between being thoughtful and being indecisive. Between waiting wisely and delaying responsibility. Transparency is required when action is imminent, when others are depending on your decision, and when trust is at stake. Leadership demands the courage to speak clearly when the moment arrives.

The Squeak

Discretion protects preparation. Transparency builds trust. There is a time to observe quietly and a time to speak decisively. When the moment comes to act, silence undermines confidence. Calling the lineup tells people you are ready to lead and willing to be accountable.

The Next Play

Is this a moment for continued discernment, or is it time to call the lineup?
If others are waiting on you, clarity is the play.

9th POSSESSION

Make It, Take It

Basketball Theory

In one-on-one pickup basketball, the rule is simple: make it, take it. If you score, you keep the ball. If you miss, possession changes. The game rewards execution. There are no sympathy possessions. No explanations. No excuses. If you want to keep the ball, you have to put it in the hoop.

That rule changes how you play. You value each possession more. You take responsibility for your shot selection. You understand that possession is earned, not given. Making the shot preserves control. Missing hands it over.

Life Application

Life should be lived on merit. If you want something, earn it. Stop expecting things to be handed to you simply because you want them. Effort precedes entitlement. Discipline precedes opportunity.

And here's the other side of it. If you want to take it, then make it. Take the shot. Take the risk. Take responsibility. Opportunities don't reward hesitation. They reward action backed by preparation.

Hardwood Insight

Players who understand make it, take it don't waste possessions. They play with intention because they know what's at stake.

Real-Life Parallel

Many people want results without responsibility. They want the outcome without the effort. Life doesn't work that way. Possession belongs to those who execute.

Leadership Insight

Strong leaders earn influence through consistency and competence. Authority that is assumed but not earned rarely lasts. People follow leaders they trust, and trust is built over time through preparation, reliability, and results. Titles may grant position, but credibility is earned through performance. Leaders who consistently show up, do the work, and deliver under pressure gain influence that does not need to be demanded. Earned authority carries weight because it is rooted in proof, not position.

The Squeak

Earn your possession. Nothing meaningful is handed to you simply because you want it. In basketball, you earn the ball by being ready, dependable, and useful to the team. In life and leadership, the same principle applies. Opportunity follows preparation. Influence follows responsibility. When you earn your possession, you respect the game, the people around you, and the moment you have been given.

The Next Play

What are you expecting to receive right now that you have not yet earned through preparation, consistency, or responsibility?
What would change if you focused less on entitlement and more on readiness?
Step up. Do the work. Earn the possession, and then make the play.

10th POSSESSION

Take Over the Game

Basketball Theory

There comes a moment in every game when someone has to step up. The clock is winding down. The defense tightens. The moment demands a play. Some players shrink. Others defer. But the great ones want the ball. They don't guarantee success, but they accept responsibility.

Taking over the game doesn't always mean scoring. Sometimes it's a stop, a rebound, a smart pass, or calming the team down. What matters is ownership. You don't hide in the moment. You engage it.

Life Application

Life has defining moments too. Situations where waiting is no longer an option. Moments when responsibility calls your name. Taking over your life means owning outcomes instead of blaming circumstances. It means stepping forward instead of watching someone else decide your future.

Hardwood Insight

Players who avoid big moments rarely grow. They stay comfortable, protected by distance from responsibility. But players who step into pressure gain something valuable every time, regardless of the outcome. Confidence is not built by watching. It is built by experience. Big moments reveal preparation, courage, and character, and those who embrace them develop the trust to handle the next one.

Real-Life Parallel

Many people live on the sidelines of their own lives, waiting for permission, perfect conditions, or someone else to lead. They observe, critique, and delay while opportunities pass. Progress begins when you accept responsibility for the direction you are headed. Growth requires participation. You do not move forward by spectating your own potential.

Leadership Insight

Strong leaders do not wait to be pushed into action. They recognize when leadership is required and respond accordingly. They act even when the outcome is uncertain and the risk is real. Leadership is not about certainty. It is about responsibility. When others hesitate, leaders step forward.

The Squeak

Be accountable. Accountability is the moment you stop pointing outward and start owning what happens next. It is the decision to say, "This is mine to handle." Teams trust leaders who accept responsibility, especially when the moment is uncomfortable. Accountability is not blame. It is ownership.

The Next Play

Where in your life is it time to stop watching and start leading? What situation is waiting for you to step up instead of stand by? Take responsibility. Enter the moment. Make the play

GAME CHANGING PLAY

Chip Away

Big deficits don't get erased with one play. They disappear slowly.

When a team is down big, panic is the enemy. Players start forcing shots. They rush possessions. They try to make something spectacular happen instead of doing what actually works. And the hole gets deeper. The teams that come back understand a different truth. You don't chase the scoreboard. You win the next possession. Then the next one. You get a stop. You secure a rebound. You take a good shot. You knock down free throws. Drain a couple of wide open threes. Little by little, momentum shifts. A twenty-point deficit becomes fifteen. Fifteen becomes ten. And suddenly, the pressure flips — and it's a new game, baby!

Comebacks are built by teams willing to chip away.

The discipline to chip away requires composure. It requires trust in the process. It requires patience when the clock says you should be desperate. The best teams don't look for one big play. They look for consistent execution. They understand that games are not won in a moment. They're won possession by possession.

Life works the same way.

Most people quit because the problem feels too big. The debt feels overwhelming. The relationship feels broken beyond repair. The health issue feels permanent. The mistake feels final. So they either panic or shut down. But life doesn't change all at once. It changes incrementally. One decision at a time. One habit at a time. One disciplined step at a time.

You don't fix everything today. You don't need to. You just need to win **this** possession.

Chipping away means staying methodical when emotions say rush. It means staying faithful when progress feels slow. It means choosing consistency over intensity. The people who win in life aren't the ones who make the biggest moves. They're the ones who keep making the right ones, long after the excitement wears off.

Momentum is deceptive. It feels sudden when it arrives, but it's always been building quietly in the background. Every good decision stacks. Every small win compounds. And eventually, what once felt impossible becomes manageable, then achievable, then real.

The mistake is believing you have to get it all back at once. You don't. That mindset leads to reckless decisions and unnecessary losses. Wisdom understands that progress earned slowly lasts longer than progress forced quickly.

Games are not won by one big play. They're won possession by possession.

That's why *Squeaky Sneakers: Life Lessons Learned on the Hardwood* isn't written in chapters. It's written in possessions. Because life isn't lived in chapters either. It's lived the same way the game is played, possession by possession, day by day, decision by decision, moment by moment.

When you commit to chipping away, pressure eases, clarity returns, and hope becomes practical again.

That's a game changer.

FREE THROWS

Don't Blame the Refs

Basketball Theory

Referees are part of the game. Some calls go your way. Some don't. Complaining after every whistle doesn't change the call. It distracts you from the next play, drains your energy, and often puts you out of position defensively. Great players understand this. They play through missed calls. They adjust. They focus on what they can control.

The scoreboard never asks who the refs were.

Life Application

Blaming external factors is a shortcut that leads nowhere. When things don't go your way, it's tempting to assign fault instead of taking responsibility. But growth requires ownership. Complaining may feel justified in the moment, but it never produces progress.

Hardwood Insight

Coaches hate ref-blaming because it signals a loss of focus. The whistle has already blown. The call has already been made. Energy spent arguing is energy stolen from execution. While players are busy reacting emotionally, the game continues to move forward. Teams that dwell on officiating lose rhythm, composure, and competitive edge. The fastest way to fall behind is to argue about what you cannot change instead of adjusting to what is happening.

Real-Life Parallel

Life is full of unfair moments, bad breaks, and circumstances outside your control. Not every outcome will feel just, and not every situation will play out the way you hoped. Fixating on what went wrong keeps you stuck in reaction mode. Maturity shows up when you stop protesting reality and start adapting to it. Progress comes from response, not complaint.

Leadership Insight

Strong leaders do not point fingers. They take responsibility for outcomes, even when conditions are not ideal. Ownership builds credibility because it signals composure, accountability, and strength. Excuses may protect ego in the moment, but they destroy trust over time. Leaders who own the moment, regardless of circumstance, earn the right to lead the next one.

The Squeak

Control what you can control. You may not control the call, the conditions, or the environment, but you always control your effort, attitude, and response. When you focus on what is within your reach, you regain clarity and momentum. Control restores composure, and composure creates opportunity.

The Next Play

Where have you been blaming circumstances instead of owning your response?
What would change if you redirected that energy toward execution instead of explanation?
Let it go. Refocus. Play on.

Basketball Theory

Whether you are putting up shots alone, grinding through intense shooting drills, practicing free throws, or just fooling around in the gym, there is a simple rule seasoned players live by. Never leave the gym on a miss. Seeing the last shot go in matters more than people realize. It is a small win, but it conditions your mind to finish well. Ending a session with success reinforces confidence, rhythm, and belief. It also sets the tone for how you return the next day. Players who finish strong walk out of the gym encouraged, not defeated.

Life Application

Life is shaped by how moments end. Conversations, workdays, projects, seasons, and even difficult stretches leave an imprint based on their closing moments. Ending well does not erase the struggle that came before it, but it reframes it. A small win at the end of a hard stretch restores momentum and renews motivation. How you finish today often determines how you show up tomorrow.

Hardwood Insight

Good shooters understand rhythm and confidence. They know that repetition builds skill, but finishing on a make builds belief. Walking out of the gym after seeing the ball go through the net reinforces trust in your work and enthusiasm for the next session. The last rep lingers.

Real-Life Parallel

Many people stop when they are tired, frustrated, or discouraged. But ending on a positive note, even a small one, changes the emotional residue of the experience. A kind word after a tough conversation. A completed task after a long day. A moment of gratitude after disappointment. Small finishes matter because they shape how the moment is remembered.

Leadership Insight

Strong leaders are intentional about endings. They close meetings with clarity. They finish projects with follow-through. They leave people encouraged, not confused. Leaders who understand the power of finishing well create environments where people want to return, re-engage, and give effort again tomorrow.

The Squeak

Never leave the gym on a miss. How you finish trains your mindset. A made shot at the end signals discipline, confidence, and respect for the work. Endings matter because they prepare you for what comes next.

The Next Play

Where do you need to create a better finish today, even if it is small? What final action would allow you to walk away encouraged instead of discouraged?
Finish well so you are ready to return with confidence tomorrow.

FINAL BUZZER

It Was A Good Run

Basketball Theory

Eventually, there comes a moment in every hooper's life when the game keeps moving, but your role changes. It doesn't come with an announcement. There's no ceremony. Sometimes it comes quietly. Other times it comes bluntly.

"Yo Unc, you mind sitting this one out so we can pick this guy up?"

I was around 39-40. The guy who next picked me up for his crew. I was warming up, getting loose, doing what I had always done. Then a guy half my age walked into the gym. He looked like a real player. And apparently, he was, because in a matter of moments, I was replaced.

Dropped. Just like that.

I agreed. Grabbed what little pride I had left. Went home.

I haven't played basketball since.

My time in the light was up. And that's okay.

Basketball has a way of telling the truth. It lets you know when it's your turn to play, and it lets you know when it's time to step aside. The game doesn't apologize. It doesn't explain. It just keeps moving.

Life Application

There comes a time in life when you have to step aside and let the next generation have it. They're ready. You blazed the trail. You put in the work. You established legacy. Now the call is different.

Stepping aside isn't quitting. It's wisdom.

There is humility in knowing when to lead and dignity in knowing when to let go. Life isn't about holding on forever. It's about pouring in deeply and then watching others carry it forward.

All good things eventually come to an end.

Hardwood Insight

Great veterans don't cling to minutes. They understand seasons. They mentor, encourage, and make room.

Real-Life Parallel

In careers, families, leadership, and influence, roles evolve. Refusing to step aside when your season has passed doesn't preserve relevance. It diminishes it.

Leadership Insight

Strong leaders build successors. They don't fear being replaced. They prepare others to thrive beyond them.

The Squeak

Finish with dignity. Walk away with your head held high.

The Next Play

Where is life asking you to release the floor and let someone else have it? Do it with humility, gratitude, and your dignity intact. It was a good run.

POST GAME SPEECH

Cherish The Moments

Seasons end. Legs slow down. One day you lace up your sneakers for the last time, and you do not realize it until much later. What once felt ordinary becomes sacred in hindsight. The practices. The games. The laughter. The sweat. The sound of squeaky sneakers echoing across a hardwood floor.

Those moments never come back. You only get to remember them.

Life works the same way. We all get older. Seasons change. Children grow. Roles shift. Opportunities come and go. One day you wake up and realize that what you are living in right now will someday be a memory.

So do not rush past what matters. Do not live so focused on what is next that you miss what is now. Presence is a decision, and it is one of the purest forms of gratitude.

Veteran players do not miss the conditioning or the pressure. They miss the moments. The locker room conversations. The shared struggle. The feeling of belonging.

At the end of life, people rarely wish they worked more. They wish they noticed more. They wish they slowed down more. They wish they cherished what they had while they had it.

Ball really is life, not because the game lasts forever, but because it teaches you how to live while it lasts.

Slow down when you need to. Be present where you are. Cherish the moments. Because one day, they will be all you have left.

GRAB YOUR BAG. LET'S GET OUTTA HERE.

A Letter to the Game

Dear Basketball,

I don't remember the exact day you entered my life, but I remember the moment you took over my heart.

You showed up quietly at first. A driveway. A playground. A gym with dusty floors and wooden backboards. Back then, I didn't know you would become a lifelong companion. I just knew I wanted to keep coming back. I wanted to be in the gym. I wanted to run the floor. I wanted to hear the sounds that told me the game was alive.

You gave me joy before I understood responsibility. You gave me discipline before I understood purpose. You gave me confidence before I knew who I was.

When I was young, I made you an idol, and you never complained when I grew older and took you off the pedestal because I met Jesus Christ and fell in love with Him. You simply stayed in your proper place and continued to serve as a teacher instead of trying to be a god.

You taught me how to work. You taught me how to lose without embarrassing myself. You taught me how to win with humility. You taught me that effort matters, that preparation shows, and that nothing meaningful comes without sacrifice.

You introduced me to people who shaped my life. You opened doors I did not know existed.

Because of you, I learned about teamwork. I learned about humility. I learned about leadership. I learned how to be coached and how to coach others. I learned how to listen, how to speak up, and how to take responsibility when the moment demanded it.

You were there when life was simple, and you stayed when life became complicated. You gave me a place to belong when I needed it most. A gym. A run. A familiar rhythm when everything else felt uncertain.

Even now, long after the lights have dimmed and the seasons have changed, you are still with me. In memories. In lessons. In the way I see the world. In the way I approach life.

You never promised forever. You never owed me anything. And yet, you gave me more than I could ever repay.

Thank you for the joy. Thank you for the lessons. Thank you for the journey. Thank you for staying with me, even after I stepped away.

You will always be part of who I am.

And I am forever grateful.